Josh the Flyer

Josh the Flyer

*Josh van der Flier
Irish Sporting Legend*

Paul O'Flynn

Gill Books

Gill Books
Hume Avenue
Park West
Dublin 12
www.gillbooks.ie

Gill Books is an imprint of M.H. Gill & Co.

Text © Paul O'Flynn 2023

978 07171 9589 3

Edited by Natasha Mac a'Bháird
Proofread by Sally Vince

Printed and bound in Great Britain by Clays Ltd, Elcograf S.p.A.

This book is typeset in 12/18pt Tahoma.

For permission to reproduce artwork, the author and publisher gratefully acknowledge the following:
© Adobe Stock/longquattro

The paper used in this book comes from the wood pulp of managed forests. For every tree felled, at least one tree is planted, thereby renewing natural resources.

All rights reserved.
No part of this publication may be copied, reproduced or transmitted in any form or by any means, without written permission of the publishers.

This book has been produced in accordance with guidelines provided by Dyslexia Ireland.

A CIP catalogue record for this book is available from the British Library.

5 4 3 2 1

Author's Note

This book is based on Josh van der Flier's life and career. It would be impossible for me to go back in time and listen in to all of the conversations with Josh that have taken place over the years, so I have had to imagine them. I also haven't actually been in the dressing rooms or Josh's home or inside his head, because that would just be weird. However, all of the scores and matches are real and all of Josh's achievements mentioned in the book are factual. He really is one of the hardest working rugby players ever.

About the Author

Paul O'Flynn is an RTÉ News and Sport presenter and journalist. He is a graduate of DCU, with a BA in Journalism and an MA in International Relations. Paul is a keen sportsperson and amateur swimmer, and in 2018 he was the winner of the Liffey Swim. This is his third Irish Sporting Legends biography, following *Go, Johnny, Go!* and *King Henry.*

Chapter 1

Grand Slam

Beep Beep Beep!

The morning alarm sounded loudly on Josh's phone, but he was already wide awake. How could he not be? He reached across the bed to turn it off, flipped the phone in his hand and looked at the screen. 7 a.m. Saturday, 18 March. This was it. The moment he'd been waiting for. Ireland v. England in the Six Nations. A Grand Slam decider. One of the biggest days in Irish rugby history.

Josh the Flyer

Ireland had already beaten Wales, France, Italy and Scotland. Now it came down to this. A win over their biggest rivals, England, would see Ireland crowned Grand Slam champions. It was something that had only happened three times in more than a hundred years. And Ireland had never won a Grand Slam in front of their home fans in Dublin. Josh could already feel the butterflies in his stomach.

Dublin was buzzing with excitement. It was the day after St Patrick's Day and everyone was talking about the game. Josh could feel the energy even inside the hotel. He was calm and focused. But his nerves were starting to grow.

By afternoon, it was time. The bus rolled up and Josh and his teammates jumped on board. It had been painted green specially for the occasion. TEAM OF US was written in huge white letters along the side. Josh sat in his usual seat and calmly looked out of the window. His heart was beating a little faster now.

Grand Slam

Fans were starting to make their way to the stadium, decked out in green jerseys, hats and scarves. Laughing, joking and singing songs. Police motorbikes led the bus along the short route to the stadium, blasting their sirens for all to hear. As the bus squeezed along Londonbridge Road, around the corner from the stadium, neighbours came out of their houses. An old man stopped cutting his grass to watch. A little girl with green ribbons in her hair stood beside her baby brother and waved. A teenage boy blew a trumpet. Josh took it all in. The whole of Ireland had stopped to watch this match. It meant everything.

The bus pulled into the Aviva Stadium and drove down the tunnel to the dressing room entrance. A special place where not many people ever got to go.

'Let's go, boys!' screamed winger James Lowe as they rose from their seats. He was already excited.

Some players kept their headphones on, listening to music. Others stayed relaxed and

Josh the Flyer

chatted. Josh remained quiet. He was focused on what he needed to do on the pitch.

As the clock ticked down to kick-off, the dressing room was full of activity. Players tying their laces, taping their hands and stretching their muscles. Coach Andy Farrell arrived for a last-minute team talk.

'This is it, boys!' yelled the tough Englishman.

Farrell was tall and strong with a big broad back and a jet-black beard. He had a loud, deep voice and could be quite scary at times. But the players loved him.

'I'm so proud of everything you've achieved so far,' he said. 'But it means nothing if you don't win today. The stadium is full of your family and friends. The people you grew up with. Your old coaches and teammates. Players who didn't make it. And thousands of people you've never met.'

Josh could feel the hairs standing up on the back of his neck. He was so pumped up for the game, he felt he could burst through the

Grand Slam

dressing room wall. He just wanted to get onto the pitch.

'An entire nation is behind you and you're representing them today,' continued the coach, jabbing his finger into his hand. 'Do them proud. Give it your all. That's all I can ever ask. When the final whistle blows, make sure you've given every bit of energy, everything you have.'

It was a spine-tingling speech.

Josh lifted his number 7 jersey from the bench and pulled it over his head. He was used to playing big matches for Ireland. He tried to calm his nerves and pretend it was just like any other game. But deep down inside he knew it wasn't. He thought of all the hard work he'd done to get where he was. He had earned the right to wear this jersey. It was all for this.

He looked around him. Ireland's inspirational captain Johnny Sexton was going through some last-minute plays. Prop Andrew Porter was smacking players on the back, getting ready for action.

Josh the Flyer

'Come on, boys!' roared hooker Dan Sheehan as he bounced a ball.

It was showtime!

The sound of studs scraped the floor of the tunnel as the players made their way towards the pitch. They could hear a wave of noise from the stadium. Fifty thousand fans bursting with excitement. Fireworks crackling and music blaring on the sound system.

Here they come. And hear the roar!

Josh looked up at a sea of green shirts as he walked onto the perfect Lansdowne Road pitch. A wall of noise crashed around him. But he felt calm. The players lined up along the red carpet and shook hands with the president. Then came the national anthems. Pin-drop silence for England's 'God Save the Queen'. And then 50,000 soaring voices for 'Amhrán na bhFiann'. Josh pulled on his famous red scrum cap and tied up the straps. The referee blew the whistle. The game was on!

But England had come to spoil the party. They wanted to stop Ireland winning a Grand

Grand Slam

Slam. And they made the better start. Just minutes in, their kicker Owen 'Faz' Farrell stepped up for the first penalty of the match.

Up go the flags. England have the points!

Faz soon added another try and the home crowd began to get edgy. England were 6–0 in front. It wasn't the start Ireland wanted. But there was still plenty of time.

'Don't panic, lads,' roared Josh to his teammates. 'Stick to the process!'

So that's exactly what they did. And soon they had a penalty of their own. Johnny Sexton lined it up, but this was no ordinary kick. Ireland's captain was about to become the all-time leading points scorer in the Six Nations. If he was feeling the pressure, he didn't show it. Calm as ever, he slotted the ball right between the posts.

'Yes, Sexto!' Josh pumped his fist. They were back in the game.

Before long Ireland had a lineout in a dangerous place. Josh knew this was a huge

Josh the Flyer

chance. The lineout was an important part of his job and they put hours of practice into getting it just right. The forwards gathered in a huddle. James Ryan barked out the instructions. Josh knew exactly what he had to do.

Hooker Dan Sheehan wiped the sweat from his hands, picked his spot and threw the ball in. A perfect spiral high into the sky, where the giant James Ryan leapt to catch it with both hands, quickly slipping it to Josh. It all happened in the blink of an eye and England were surprised.

Van Der Flier ... Back inside ... Sheehan ... Gap opens up ... Sheehaaaaannnnn!

Ireland have the opening try. And the place has gone wild!

'Yessssssss!' yelled Josh. He was first in to celebrate. 'What a finish, Danno!'

'Wouldn't have happened without your perfect pass, Josh!'

It was a tough, tense match with neither side giving an inch. Then, just before half-time, came a moment that changed the game.

Grand Slam

Ireland's full-back Hugo Keenan was chasing a loose bouncing ball when he felt a blow to his head.

Owwwww!

England's Freddie Steward charged into him with his shoulder. The crowd groaned. It looked bad. Hugo was shaken but OK. The referee wasn't happy though. He sent Steward off for dangerous play.

A red card! England are down to 14 men!

It was a huge opportunity. But no matter what Ireland did, they couldn't seem to score again. They were nervous and kept dropping the ball. Faz kicked another penalty for England and suddenly they were just a point behind. Johnny was getting angry and was barking at the referee. The crowd were getting restless. Josh started to wonder if his Grand Slam dreams were about to crumble.

Then, with 20 minutes to go, Ireland got their chance. A scrum five metres out from the English line. Josh knew this was their moment.

Josh the Flyer

He flexed his muscles and crouched down with the Ireland pack.

'Big squeeze, boys,' roared scrum-half Jamison Gibson-Park.

Josh knew Ireland needed the scrum of their lives.

'Crouch ... Bind ... Set!' called the referee.

Josh pushed with all his might. The England pack stepped backwards, the scrum collapsed and the ball popped out. Gibson-Park quickly fizzed a fast pass to Bundee Aki. Bundee smashed into the English defenders and fell to the ground. Josh was first to the ball and forcefully shoved the English players out of the way. The ball came back again. This time Josh threw a dummy run that fooled England's defence. Bundee had the ball once more and popped it to Robbie Henshaw in some space. The crowd roared in anticipation. Everyone watching at home held their breath.

'Go!' yelled Josh to Robbie. But Henshaw was already over the line. It had all happened in a flash.

Grand Slam

Yessssss! Robbie Henshaw! The power and precision of Ireland!

A superb try. But Josh and his teammates wanted more.

Soon they were deep into England's half again. Mack Hansen sent Dan Sheehan clear with a perfect pass. Josh tracked the move all the way, hitting the England defence every time they came near. He was a bundle of energy, even in the closing moments of the game. He never got tired. His hard work suddenly opened up some space. And Ireland were quick to take advantage.

Conan ... To Sheehan ... Ohhh, that is wonderful! Try number two for Dan Sheehan!

Ireland were 15 points ahead now. But England still didn't give up. A rolling maul powered the ball all the way over the try line. The men in white were right back in it.

'Nooooo!' thought Josh. 'It's too late to let this slip now!'

But there was one more twist in the story of this epic encounter. The men in green pushed

Josh the Flyer

their tired bodies into attack one last time. Josh, as ever, was right at the heart of it, leading by example. And, eventually, England gave way.

Ireland are looking to put a cherry on top. Rob Herring! There it is ... The winning try!

It's a greenwash Grand Slam on St Patrick's weekend!

The crowd was in full voice now. 'The Fields of Athenry' rang out around the stands. Josh took a moment to look around and take it all in. At last, the referee blew the final whistle, and the game was over.

Ireland are the Grand Slam champions!

Josh almost fell to his knees with exhaustion. Instead, he collapsed into the arms of his giant tattooed teammate, Andrew Porter.

'We did it, Ports,' was all he could say. He was too tired to talk anymore.

The fans danced and sang, the players hugged and clapped each other on the back. Josh congratulated his teammates one by one.

Grand Slam

Together they had done something no Irish team had done before. It was special.

They each received their medals. And then the moment they'd all been waiting for. Captain Sexton stepped up to lift the glistening Six Nations Trophy, standing in front of Josh and smiling, before raising it high into the Dublin night sky.

Johnny handed the trophy to Josh.

'You're the man, Sexto!' said Josh.

'Not bad for an old man!' replied Johnny with a grin.

As the celebrations went on, Josh broke away to find his family. His new wife Sophie, his mam and dad, his brother and one of his sisters, his uncles and aunts, cousins and even his grandad George, were all there to watch this special moment. His parents had tears in their eyes as they hugged him.

'Thanks for everything,' said Josh to his parents.

'You always told me I could do it, Dad,' he said, smiling from ear to ear.

Josh the Flyer

His grandad gave Josh a hug. 'I'm so proud of you,' he said.

Josh's mam and dad, his grandparents and all his family had been with him all the way on his special journey from schoolboy to Grand Slam champion.

But his story started a long time before that famous night in Dublin. It began in County Wicklow, back in 1993.

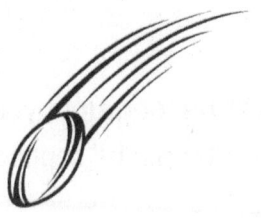

Chapter 2

Dutch Disciple

Joshua Dirk van der Flier was born on 25 April 1993, in Holles Street Hospital in Dublin. He was a bouncing, big-eyed boy, full of beans, with a lovely soft sprinkling of tiny blond hairs. His mam and dad, Olly and Dirk, were so delighted.

'Isn't he beautiful?' said his mother, with a tear in her eye.

The baby opened his eyes and smiled.

'I think he's a mammy's boy already,' joked his dad.

Josh the Flyer

'Sure, it won't be long until you have him down the rugby pitch!' replied his mam, laughing.

Josh's dad loved rugby. He was a handy player himself back in his day. A fast, strong winger who played for the Leinster under-21s, Old Wesley and Wicklow.

'Actually, now that you say it, I got him a little present,' said his dad, opening a bag.

He took out a tiny, soft rugby ball. Blue and white with 'Gilbert' written across it. Just like the real thing.

'Oh, Dirk,' laughed Josh's mam.

His dad leaned over the cot and placed the rugby ball gently beside the little baby.

'Now, Josh,' he whispered into his son's ear, 'I hope this little ball brings you luck in life. And, you never know, you might just play for Ireland someday!'

Rugby was the talk of the town around that time. The Ireland team wasn't particularly good back in 1993. But just days before Josh was born, they had a famous win over England at

Dutch Disciple

Lansdowne Road. The winning try was scored by a legendary player called Mick Galwey, who powered over the line with an England player dragging his shirt.

Mick Galwey's in ... Mick Galwey seals it for Ireland!

It was the first time in seven years that Ireland had beaten England and the fans went wild. They stormed the pitch and joined the celebrations. Mick Galwey's sister made it onto the pitch to congratulate him, chased all the way by the stadium security!

It was a crazy game that lived long in the memory of those who saw it. Especially Josh's mam and dad. They were watching it on television as they waited for Josh to be born. His mam was certain she felt the baby kick inside her as Mick Galwey crashed over the try line. Maybe it was written in the stars, she thought, that the little baby about to be born would one day make his own mark in the history of Irish rugby, helping Ireland to another famous win over England.

Josh the Flyer

A nurse came to check on Josh.

'He's gorgeous,' she said as she looked at the tiny name tag tied around Josh's wrist.

'Joshua ... Dirk. Van. Der ... Fly-er?' she read out loud, a little unsure how to say his name.

'Josh for short,' said his dad. 'And it's van der Fleer. That's how you say it. It's a Dutch name.' He smiled at the nurse.

Josh's grandparents on his dad's side were both born in the Netherlands. His grandad, Johannes, was from Amsterdam and his granny, Joke, was from the Hague. They moved to Ireland back in the 1950s. In Dutch names, the letter J is pronounced like Y so Josh's grandparents had to teach their new friends and neighbours how to say their names! They first lived in Finglas in Dublin, before moving to Wicklow where Johannes set up a radiator factory in the centre of the town. He often joked that he found living in Ireland so cold, he had to make his own radiators for heat!

Josh's other grandfather, George Strong, grew up in Kilkenny. When George got older

Dutch Disciple

he moved to Waterford. He would cycle more than 100 kilometres to Kilkenny and back just to play for the local rugby club. Josh's uncle, Dermot Strong, was a former captain of the Old Wesley Club in Dublin too.

So it was no surprise that Josh followed his family's footsteps into rugby. His family background gave him the perfect mix of hard work, strength, and a love of the game, which set him on the path to becoming a rugby superstar of the future.

His parents wrapped a blanket around their little bundle of joy, with his squished-up rugby ball tucked under his arm, and prepared to leave the hospital. They couldn't wait to bring Josh home to meet his older brother, Johan, back in their family home in Wicklow.

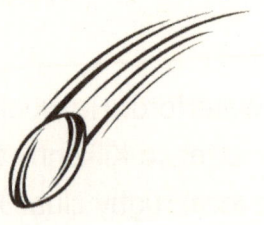

Chapter 3

Wicklow Way

Josh was able to throw a rugby ball long before he could walk. But that was no wonder because he loved all the same things as his older brother Johan. And Johan was rugby mad, just like their dad.

Johan was much taller than Josh (he would grow up to be six foot seven!). But that didn't stop the younger brother from having a go. Even though he was small for his age, Josh was starting to show his bravery. Johan loved

Wicklow Way

to push his younger brother around. But Josh would always come back for more. It was great fun!

The pair had bags of energy, but they broke their mother's heart with their antics. They were always climbing, pushing, shoving, running and jumping. They usually had dirty knees too.

'Boys, be careful!' she would roar. 'I don't want to end up in hospital with you.'

But it was no good. The two boys were too lively. When it came to sports, there was just no stopping them.

Josh and Johan spent all their time outside. They didn't have a television in their house, so they passed hours every day playing in the garden. Everywhere Johan and Josh went they would have a ball in their hands. It didn't matter where they were or what was going on. And most of the time it was a rugby ball.

The boys loved to watch their dad in action too. Dirk played for the local club, Wicklow Town, and was one of the toughest tacklers

Josh the Flyer

anybody there had ever seen. Johan and Josh watched his every move. When they got home, they would re-live the matches in their back garden. Josh would pull on his dad's jersey, even though it came down to his toes, and pretend he was his dad playing the game.

Dirk van der Flier catches the ball in clear space ... There's nobody near him ... It's a try! A try for Wicklow! There's just no stopping the flying Dutchman!

Josh would imagine the commentary in his head as he ran around the garden in his oversized jersey. His mam, dad and Johan watched, laughing. Josh also loved trying to wrestle his dad to the ground. And when he went back inside, he'd try out his tackle technique on the sofa. He was already dreaming of one day playing at the highest level.

'Josh! I hope you're not jumping on the furniture again,' his mam would shout as she made the dinner.

'No, Mam! I just fell,' Josh would fib, with Johan laughing beside him.

Wicklow Way

Before he even started primary school, Josh was already learning the basics of rugby. His dad taught him how to tackle, catch, kick and pass. Josh was an eager student. But the most important lesson was in the mind. And he learned that from his grandad.

'You can be whatever you want to be, Josh,' his grandad Johannes told him. 'But first you must work hard. That's the only way to be successful. It doesn't matter if you're too small, too slow, or not as strong as the others. Listen to your teachers and coaches. Do what they say. Train hard. Practise your skills every day. Whether it's sport or in school, the only way to get what you want is to work hard for it.'

Josh listened to every word.

'We're van der Fliers,' continued his grandad. 'That's what we do! We work hard.'

'OK, Grandad!' said Josh with a smile.

It was a lesson he would never forget to apply.

Before long, the van der Flier family grew again. Josh now had two younger sisters,

Josh the Flyer

Kirstin and Julie. They were also sports mad and the games in the garden they all had together were some of the best days in Josh's life. It was mostly rugby, but sometimes tennis and cricket too. Julie would grow up to play cricket for Ireland. So Josh wasn't the only sports star in the family.

Sometimes, they would leave the garden, sneaking off for adventures when nobody was looking. One day, the circus came to Wicklow Town. Everybody was excited, especially Josh, Johan and their sisters. They saw the brightly coloured circus tent, the animals, including lions and bears, the clowns and acrobats. Josh watched the trucks arrive with his eyes wide open in amazement. He had to have a closer look.

'Let's go have a peep,' said Josh to Johan.

'I dunno, Josh. We're not supposed to,' replied Johan.

'Come on! Nobody will notice,' said Josh, laughing. He was already on his way.

'OK, wait! We'll all go!' said Johan.

Wicklow Way

So Josh, Johan, their sisters and cousins all headed off down the road to try to sneak into the circus.

It was so much fun. They had to make their way in unnoticed. Josh was a little worried they'd be caught and get in big trouble.

They climbed over a fence and crouched behind some trees, hiding. Josh's heart was pounding fast. The circus tent was right in front of them now. Red, white and blue canvas, stretching high into the sky. It was the biggest tent Josh had ever seen.

They took a few more quiet steps towards the edge of the tent and lay down on the ground. Josh held his breath. They were well hidden in the long grass. But still he worried someone might see.

Johan pulled up the side of the tent. And Josh peeped under. It was magical. He could see elephants, acrobats and clowns all practising. The lights were sparkling and there was loud music playing. Suddenly, Josh got the fright of his life.

Josh the Flyer

Grrrrrrrrrrrrrrrrr!

A huge roar erupted in Josh's ear. He nearly jumped out of his skin. He pulled his head back out from the tent and jumped to his feet. Then he ran for his life. He was always a very fast runner.

'What was that?' shouted Johan.

'I think it was a lion!' said Josh, panting. He was out of breath.

When the coast was clear they all collapsed to the ground, laughing. Josh, his brother and sisters and cousins.

'Was it really a lion?' asked Kirstin.

'Well, maybe it was just a circus guy playing a trick,' said Josh, wiping the sweat from his brow. 'But I wasn't hanging around to find out!'

***

Johan was playing for the Wicklow under-8s rugby team and his dad was the coach. Josh was only five, but he tagged along, watching from the sideline as the bigger boys played. He loved everything about it. The smell of

Wicklow Way

the grass, the floodlights sparkling on a cold winter's night, the players sliding in the mud. He couldn't wait to start.

Then one night his dad asked him to join in.

'Well, if you're going to just stand there watching, you might as well take part,' he said as he winked at Josh. 'But don't tell your mother you were playing with the big boys!'

Josh was in heaven. The cones, the drills and the tackle bags – it was all so exciting. It was his first taste of real rugby and there was no going back. The only problem was he couldn't play any proper matches. He was still three years too young to be allowed on the team!

When Josh wasn't playing sports, he loved watching them on TV. His grandmother, Joke, lived right next door and luckily for Josh, she had a TV. Josh was close to his grandparents, so he popped in to see them all the time.

Joke was a big sports fan too and made sure all the family stayed in touch with their Dutch roots. One time, she bought Josh the

Josh the Flyer

jersey for the Dutch national soccer team as a present. It was bright orange and Josh loved wearing it. Anytime Ireland weren't playing, Josh supported the Dutch.

The family played many games of football or rugby in the garden, making up funny names for their teams. One game with Josh's cousins went on for hours. His team was called Lasagne, after his favourite dinner. They wore Dutch jerseys. His cousins' team was Apple Pie, after their favourite dessert. They wore green for Ireland. After a long day in the sun, they called it a draw. Lasagne 20, Apple Pie 20 was the final score!

One summer, in 1998, the soccer World Cup was on in France. The Dutch had a talented team with players like Dennis Bergkamp, Patrick Kluivert and Marc Overmars. Bergkamp was Josh's favourite player. He was so skilful and creative. He had outstanding vision and could do things no other player would even dream of trying. In one match, a quarter-final against Argentina, he scored one of the most beautiful goals in the history of the World Cup.

Josh was watching the match at home with his family, wearing his Dutch jersey. His granny and grandad were watching too, cheering on their home country.

The match was level at 1–1 and looked certain to go to extra time. But suddenly Dutch defender Frank de Boer played a long left-footed pass, straight over Argentina's defence. It looked to be going out of play. It was impossible to control. But not for Bergkamp. He caught the ball on his right foot straight out of the air and stopped it dead. He then flicked it back inside the hapless Argentina defender with the same movement. People around the world gasped in awe. Josh's granny let out a scream: 'Wow!'

Then it got even better. Bergkamp shifted his body to the left before curling a screamer right into the back of the net.

Bergkaaaaamp! A last-minute winner sends the Dutch into the semi-finals!

Josh jumped into his granny's arms.

Josh the Flyer

'Yessss!' he shouted.

'What a goal!' His granny laughed in delight.

Josh fell in love with Dennis Bergkamp that day. Even though he didn't play soccer, he loved watching skilful players in any sport. Ireland's Brian O'Driscoll was his favourite rugby player growing up and he loved New Zealand's Richie McCaw, too. He played the same position as Josh, so he watched him and tried to learn everything he could.

***

Later Josh discovered that Bergkamp played for Arsenal, so he decided to support them. He was lucky enough to be brought to London by his uncle once to see Arsenal play. It was the trip of a lifetime, and he wasn't disappointed. Arsenal won 1–0. And who scored the winning goal? Bergkamp, of course! Josh was a fan for life. That broke his dad's heart. Dirk was a Leeds fan and he had hoped Josh would follow them too. But Josh thought they weren't much good. So he decided to stick with the Gunners!

Wicklow Way

But years later, when Leeds were promoted back to the Premier League, Josh realised he had a soft spot for them too. He finally made his dad happy and decided to support Leeds as well!

Chapter 4

Hat-Trick Hero

By the age of seven, Josh was ready to play his first proper match with Wicklow. He was so excited. But there was a problem. He was still small for his age and he wasn't sure if he would be strong enough to play with the other boys.

'It's not fair,' he thought. 'Why can't I be tall like my brother?'

Josh's dad had an idea.

'The great thing about rugby is that it's a game for all shapes and sizes,' he said, putting his arm around Josh's shoulder. 'So, I think you'd make a good scrum-half. That's where the smallest players usually play.'

'What does the scrum-half do?' asked Josh.

'Well, it's one of the most important positions,' replied his dad. 'Not everyone can play there. You must be fast, strong and have an accurate pass. But, most importantly, you need brains. You must think one step ahead of all the other players.'

'Sounds good to me,' said Josh, taking on the challenge as ever. 'I think I can do it!'

Josh spent his days at Glebe National School dreaming of the big match to come. He was a quiet boy in class and never caused any trouble, although he wasn't a major fan of schoolwork. He tried to listen to his teacher during English, Irish and maths classes. But he found it hard to concentrate for too long. Usually he stared out of the window and dreamed of playing rugby.

The day of Josh's first match finally came. He woke early, polishing his boots, rolling up

Josh the Flyer

his socks and cleaning his gum shield. He packed his Wicklow jersey with pride. Red, white and black stripes, just like his dad's. Except his had number 9 on the back. He was all set.

They were playing Wicklow's rivals Greystones on the local pitch. It was a damp, cloudy morning with few people there to watch. But for Josh, it might as well have been the World Cup final. He was so excited.

The referee blew the whistle and the game was on.

Peep!

The initial stages were a bit of a mess. Josh and his teammates weren't sure what they were doing. They kept dropping the ball and running to the wrong places. Josh's dad was screaming on the sideline.

'Come on, boys! Keep your shape,' he roared.

But after a while, things started to click. All their training was coming together. Suddenly, Josh got a chance. A big Greystones forward fumbled the ball and it landed right in front of Josh. He didn't think twice. Like a flash he picked up the ball and raced to the line.

Josh van der Flier! Goes for the line. And it's a tryyyyyy! A first try in his first game!

'Yes, Joshy!' His teammates jumped on his back.

Minutes later, he was in again. The Greystones defence seemed to have fallen asleep, but Josh was wide awake. Just like his dad had told him, he stayed one step ahead. He reached down, picked up the ball and in one movement, touched down over the try line from close range.

Unbelievable ... He's scored another!

But he wasn't finished yet. Greystones came back into the match, and it was level going into the closing stages. Everyone was getting tired, including Josh. But he found the energy for one more burst.

His teammate Jack kicked the ball forward into space behind the Greystones defence. The

Josh the Flyer

race was on. Josh was first to see the chance so he had a head start. The opposing winger turned to cover but he was too late. Josh was out of sight, picking up the ball and scampering for the line.

'Go on, Josh!' cheered his dad from the sideline.

Josh crossed the line and fell to the ground.

Three tries! A hat-trick in his first ever game! This boy is one for the future. Josh van der Flier. Remember the name!

The game was over, and Wicklow had won. It had gone exactly how Josh had dreamed it. His teammates lifted him onto their shoulders, as the Greystones players clapped him off the pitch. He was on top of the world.

'I guess you're right, Dad,' said Josh, smiling from ear to ear. 'Maybe scrum-half IS the place for me!'

His dad patted him on the head and gave him a big thumbs-up.

Josh came home exhausted and covered in mud. His mam cooked him his favourite dinner of lasagne. He lapped it all up, had a bath and went straight to sleep, where he dreamed of the day he became Wicklow's hat-trick hero.

It didn't always go so well, though. In another memorable match, Josh's team were playing New Ross in Wexford. Josh caught the ball in the middle of the field and saw a bit of space. He ran at top speed, but two huge New Ross players were coming towards him.

They were the biggest players on the pitch. Strong and hard. But Josh thought he could beat them with speed. He kept running. The defenders closed in. The gap was narrow, but Josh put his head down and pumped his legs as fast as he could.

'I'm going to make it,' he thought. But then...
Smasssssshhh!
'Owwwwwwww!'

Josh was hit with a crunching tackle. On both sides. He was the meat in the sandwich of the two New Ross players. He hurt his knee and had to be carried off. He didn't know at the time, but one of the players that ran into him

Josh the Flyer

was a young boy called Tadhg Furlong, who would also grow up to play for Ireland. But that meant little to Josh that day as he sat on the sideline, holding an ice pack to his knee.

Chapter 5

Golden Ticket

A few years later, Josh's dad came home from work with a special surprise.

'Josh!' he called. 'Come here. I've got something to show you!'

Josh ran straight to his dad.

'What is it?' he asked excitedly.

'Go on, have a look,' said his dad, showing him two pieces of paper in his hand.

Josh grabbed them quickly. They were tickets. But for what? He didn't dare to hope.

Josh the Flyer

He turned them over and read out loud: 'Ireland v. Scotland, Lansdowne Road. 27 March 2004.' His eyes opened wide with delight.

'No way, Dad! For real?' he asked.

'Yep, son. The hottest tickets in town. We're going to the Triple Crown decider!'

Josh couldn't believe his luck. He was off to Lansdowne Road for the first time. The home of Irish rugby, where Ireland were taking on Scotland for the Triple Crown. They had already beaten Wales and England, so hopes were high. And Josh would be in the crowd of over 40,000 fans for what could be a very memorable day. He couldn't wait to tell his friends in school.

That Saturday they travelled to Dublin by train. Josh took everything in as they arrived at Lansdowne Road station. The place was heaving with Ireland fans decked in green, shouting and singing. The Scottish fans brought great colour too, wearing kilts and playing the bagpipes. It was a special atmosphere.

Golden Ticket

Inside the ground, Josh could hardly see a thing. It was packed and he was getting more squashed by the minute. So his dad lifted him up on his shoulders. At least there was one good thing about being small and light.

'Perfect!' he thought. 'Now I have the best view in the house.'

He sang the national anthem along with the crowd, as loudly as his voice could manage. And then it was time for kick-off.

Ireland hadn't won a Triple Crown for almost 20 years. But now there was real hope that a new young team might finally do the business. They had skilful players like Paul O'Connell, Anthony 'Axel' Foley, Ronan O'Gara, and Gordon D'Arcy. And above all, Brian O'Driscoll, Josh's favourite. He couldn't believe he was seeing him in the flesh.

Ireland made a nervy start. But Geordan Murphy's try just before half-time gave them a 16–9 lead. Josh loved every second. The roar of the crowd was even louder than he'd imagined. It was deafening.

Josh the Flyer

Soon Scotland were level again and Ireland were getting nervous. Was their Triple Crown dream about to die once more? Josh was biting his nails with nerves. But Ireland started to find their groove and were soon back in front.

David Wallace crashes over! Power and poise!

O'Gara slotted the conversion and finally Ireland had a cushion. Josh watched it all unfold in every detail. Before long, they scored again.

This time scrum-half Peter Stringer popped up to slide over.

A try for Ireland — and surely that's the game!

Just like Josh, Stringer was the smallest player on the pitch. But with quick thinking and speed of play, he scored the try that mattered. Josh loved watching him.

Finally, Gordon D'Arcy scored his second try to seal a historic win.

D'Arcy with the tryyyyy! And that's the Triple Crown! Ireland will party tonight!

Golden Ticket

Josh jumped up and down with the crowd.
'What a day!' He beamed at his dad.
'I'll never forget it as long as I live,' replied his dad. 'These days don't come around too often.'
Josh was on cloud nine. He'd never seen anything so exciting. From then on, playing rugby for Ireland was all he wanted to do. And on the train home he dreamed that someday, he too would win a Triple Crown for Ireland against Scotland at Lansdowne Road. A dream that surely couldn't come true. Could it?

Chapter 6

Wesley

The years spent growing up in Wicklow were the happiest of Josh's life. Playing rugby, going to matches with his dad and having fun with his brother and sisters at home. He loved every minute. But he was growing up fast and it was time for a change. He was ready for secondary school and that meant a move to Dublin to start his new life at Wesley College.

Josh's mam and dad had both been students at Wesley College. It was where they first met and later fell in love. They were both

Wesley

very sporty, winning everything on sports day. Josh's mam was one of the best hockey players in the school. She didn't like to lose! That was something Josh inherited from her.

Josh's older brother Johan had started at Wesley a few years before. So it made sense for Josh to follow in his family's footsteps and pack his bags for Wesley College.

The school was a good distance from his home in Wicklow, so Josh would board there. That meant he lived at the school during the week, sleeping in special rooms called dorms with all the other boys in his class. Then he went home on Fridays for the weekend.

At first, Josh found it really hard. He had never been away from home before and was homesick. He missed his mam and dad and his sisters, and especially having home-cooked meals. He was lonely at night-time and struggled to make new friends. But there was one thing that helped with all that. Rugby.

Rugby was a huge deal at Wesley College. It wasn't a big school. And they certainly

Josh the Flyer

weren't the best of all the strong rugby schools on the southside of Dublin. They had only ever won the Schools Senior Cup once in their history. That was way back in 1898. More than a hundred years before Josh started school there!

Only two players from the school ever went on to play rugby for Ireland. Herbert Aston in 1908 and Eric Miller in 1997. There was a special plaque inside the front door of the school with their photos, along with all the other students from the school who played sport for Ireland. There were hockey players, sailors and cricketers.

Each morning as he passed it, Josh dreamed that one day in the future his photo and the name van der Flier would be on the wall too. Little did he know that his sister Julie would beat him to it, when she played cricket for Ireland at the age of 14.

So although the school didn't have much success, rugby was an important part of life there. Every day after class, Josh and his

Wesley

friends would throw a ball around before they did their homework. And after dinner they would often head back outside for a game of tip rugby. It helped Josh settle and make friends. He formed a close bond with his classmates Danny and Peter, who were rugby-mad like Josh. They had great fun together on and off the pitch, slagging, messing and joking together all the time.

They got up to plenty of mischief too. One night, around Hallowe'en, one of the boys got his hands on some fireworks. When everyone else was in bed, they sneaked over to the window and set them off into the yard. It was chaos. There were huge bangs and bright sparks exploding all over the school grounds.

Fizz! Bang! Crash!

Josh and his friends ran for cover. Luckily, nobody was hurt. The teachers were so cross. But they never found out who did it!

As time passed, Josh settled in and started to enjoy his new life at boarding school. But he still struggled a little with schoolwork. He

Josh the Flyer

liked history, woodwork and PE. He didn't like English much, but he loved his English teacher, Mr MacMonagle. He gave Josh a love of poetry.

Josh's escape from classwork came on the rugby field. He had been one of the better players on his team in Wicklow. But this was another level. At Wesley, Josh was just an ordinary player, and he was more worried about his size now than ever. Some of the boys were huge. They were more like men. Or giants!

The sessions in the gym were fearsome and the boys would talk about the heavy weights they could bench press. Josh was nowhere near as strong as them and he doubted whether he would ever be able to compete with them for a place on the team.

The training sessions at Wesley were even more intense than at Wicklow. Things were getting serious. On the pitch they trained every day. Off it, they held team meetings discussing tactics, set-piece plays and running lines. Josh drank it all in. The more detail the better. He

Wesley

loved listening to his coaches Craig and Ian and always asked them for advice. Then he put it into practice on the pitch.

Before long, they had a big match coming up against St Gerard's in the Leinster Schools Father Godfrey Cup Final. But Josh and his teammates still had a lot to learn.

The match would be played in Donnybrook Stadium, the same place Leinster played. There was great excitement in the school. All the students were given a half day to go. They dressed up in red and blue, the colours of the school, and brought loudspeakers to make as much noise as they could. Josh's friends Danny, Greg and Peter were all on the team. It was all they had talked about for weeks.

This was Josh's first time playing in front of a big crowd. His grandad George had come to see the game, along with Josh's parents, and that made him nervous. But Wesley started the game well and Josh started to feel more relaxed. Soon they had a penalty and Greg, who was the kicker, stepped up to take it.

Josh the Flyer

A clean, crisp strike. Wesley are in front!

'Great shot, Greg. Let's go, boys!' roared Josh, as he clapped his hands to encourage his teammates.

It was a rough, tough game with Josh, Danny, Greg and Peter all getting stuck in. But that was as good as it got for Wesley. They just couldn't get any go forward ball. St Gerard's had a strong number 8 called Jack Conan. He tore Wesley to shreds, scoring the opening try.

A powerful carry from Conan! Such strength for a young man!

He was on fire that day and Josh and his teammates took a terrible beating. The game finished 39–3. Josh left the field with his tail between his legs.

'Who's that guy? The number 8?' asked Peter.

'He's a beast,' replied Josh. 'I couldn't stop him all day.'

'He'll surely play for Ireland someday,' said Greg, wiping the dirt from his face.

Wesley

'Well, I hope I never see him again,' said Josh, as he sat with his head in his hands in the dressing room.

Their coach Craig stood up.

'Hard luck, boys,' he said, as he looked around at the sad faces in front of him. 'The important thing is that you gave your best. That's all we can ask,' he reminded them gently.

'But I want you all to remember this feeling. Remember how low you feel right now. You don't ever want to feel like this on a rugby pitch again. So, let's bounce back. Let's train harder, work smarter and stick together. We'll be back!'

The players gave a half-hearted clap. Josh felt a little better after the speech. But not much. His dream of making it as a rugby player seemed further away than ever.

'If I want to make it to the top,' he thought to himself, 'then I need to make big changes.'

Chapter 7

The Boy in the Red Scrum Cap

Over the summer, a strange thing happened. Josh suddenly started to grow. Not all at once. But, slowly and surely, his body began to stretch. His legs and arms got longer, his feet and hands got bigger, his back and shoulders got broader, and his muscles became stronger. He was eating everything he could get his hands on and was still hungry all the time. He could feel his body changing day by day. This was the moment he'd been waiting for since

The Boy in the Red Scrum Cap

he was a young boy. He was finally catching up with his big brother Johan.

When Josh went back to school in September, he felt different. He felt like he fitted in with the other boys a bit more. But it was when he stepped onto the rugby pitch that he really noticed the change.

Out of nowhere, Josh was suddenly able to keep up with the big boys on the field. In the early season games, he was starting to throw himself into contact, getting stuck into rucks and making tackles. His coaches felt it was time for a chat.

'Josh, you know the scrum-half is supposed to stay out of trouble. Keep the ball moving. Don't get tackled,' said Craig, after training one day.

'I'm just enjoying the contact a bit more, Coach,' responded Josh. 'I feel I can help the team.'

'Well, that's what we were thinking,' said Craig. 'How do you fancy playing in the back row? Number 8?'

Josh the Flyer

'Wow! It's a big change,' said Josh, surprised.

'We think it's the best way to use your skills. You have so much energy. A magnificent work-rate. You're fast, fit and you've got a sixth sense for where the ball is going. Now that you're getting bigger and stronger, we think you can do it. But you have a lot to learn,' continued Craig.

'I'm up for it,' said Josh.

And that was it. He was now a back row forward and about to begin a whole new journey!

Josh was energised by the move and by his new-found strength. So he hit the gym harder than ever. He did his own research online into personal training and worked on his strength and fitness. He even risked getting in trouble just to train harder.

The school gym was locked up at night by the teachers. But some of the older boys in the school came up with a plan. When the moment was right, they managed to get their hands on a set of keys from the teacher's desk. They

The Boy in the Red Scrum Cap

knew exactly which key was for the gym, so they slipped it off the key ring and hid it. That evening they sneaked out to the local hardware shop and got a new key cut. An exact copy. Now the older boys had their own key for the gym. All the boys were delighted. They could sneak in whenever they got a chance, and the teachers would never know!

At one stage Josh was training nine sessions a week. Way too much! But he only had one thing on his mind. Becoming a rugby star. And before long his hard work paid off. He made it onto the Wesley Senior Cup team.

He made one other important change at this time too. He got himself a brand-new red scrum cap. He loved how the burning red colour stood out against the green grass of the rugby field. And best of all, it matched the Wesley school jersey. He got a bit of slagging from the lads when he started to wear it.

'What's the craic with the scrum cap, Josh?' asked Greg, laughing.

'Are you switching to Munster?' joked Peter.

Josh the Flyer

Josh didn't care. He loved it.

'The refs will be all over you,' said Greg, more seriously. 'You'll never get away with anything again!'

'Yeah, I suppose it'll make me stand out alright,' said Josh quietly.

And that's exactly what he wanted.

The Senior Cup was fast approaching. Josh was raring to go. He'd never been as prepared for a game in his life. The whole team had been working hard and training was going well. Josh had reached another level and was enjoying his role as a number 8.

Wesley were playing Catholic University School, CUS, in the semi-final in Stradbrook in Dublin. It was on TV. That's how important it was. Greg was captain of the team and he called the players in for a huddle.

'This is it, boys … Six years of school all comes down to this. Give it everything!' he said, in a clear, calm voice.

'We've done the hard work. Now trust yourselves. Trust your teammates!' said Josh,

The Boy in the Red Scrum Cap

joining in. Although he was quiet, he was becoming a leader on the team. He liked to make his voice heard.

The game was on. Wesley started well. But they were soon in trouble. A defensive mix-up gave CUS space. And their centre, David Beakey, waltzed in for a try.

'That's way too easy,' roared Josh, annoyed with himself.

Soon Greg kicked a penalty to keep them in touch. But before half-time, CUS were in again. This time prop Tadhg Doyle crashed over the try. Wesley were in trouble. They trailed 12–3 at half-time.

Josh was fuming. But he said nothing. He just let his anger simmer, hoping it would give him the power to fight back.

He played like a man possessed after the break, hitting everything that moved. He tackled himself to a standstill and got on the ball, trying to make something happen. Eventually, he got the reward his performance deserved. Wesley had a scrum well inside the CUS half.

Josh the Flyer

'Huge shove, lads!' called Josh from the back, as he fastened the strap on his red scrum cap and prepared for the push of his life.

Greg popped the ball into the scrum and the eight Wesley forwards pushed as one. The ball came back perfectly to Josh's feet. He saw his chance. Picking up the ball with one hand and pushing his opponent with the other, he used all his new-found strength. The space opened and he didn't hesitate. Off he went at speed, pumping his feet as he left the CUS defenders for dead.

What a tryyyyy! Josh van der Flier with a storming run. Power, pace and precision! Wesley are back in the game!

'Yes, Josh!' roared Peter as he patted him on the head.

Josh was delighted. But there was no time to celebrate. There was still work to do. Greg slotted the conversion. The Wesley fans, decked out in blue and red, cheered. The game couldn't be tighter between two evenly matched teams. It was 10–10 now, heading

The Boy in the Red Scrum Cap

into the closing stages. Wesley were back in the game.

Wesley knew they were on top and pushed hard for the winning score. Josh was everywhere. It was a perfect performance.

But then disaster struck.

Wesley forced a move and took too much risk. That left space out the back. And suddenly CUS were away. It was Josh that got the winning score. But not Josh van der Flier. It was CUS substitute Josh Fallon-Doran who sprinted away for the decisive try. Josh watched it happen as if it was in slow motion.

'Nooooooo!' he thought to himself, as he saw their move break down and his opponent streak away. He chased back as hard as he could. But it was no good. The damage was done. Wesley's cup dreams were over.

Josh fell to the ground. He had played the game of his life. But it wasn't enough. It was his last year in school, and he knew he would never play with most of these players again. He was so sad.

Josh the Flyer

'Well played, Josh,' said Greg, as he shook his friend's hand. 'If only the rest of us played as well as you.'

But Josh had nothing to say. He pulled off his red scrum cap and tossed it to the ground in disgust. It seemed all his hard work had come to nothing.

He had no idea that on the other side of the pitch a conversation was happening that would change his life.

A scout from the Leinster Academy had been watching the game, looking for new talent. He was wearing a long navy coat and a cap and had a small notebook in one hand and a pen in the other.

'Who's the lad in the red scrum cap?' he asked one of the coaches on the touchline.

'Oh, that's Josh. Josh van der Flier. From Wicklow. He was great today!' replied the coach.

'Are you sure that's him?' asked the scout. 'He was in with us for trials last year. He was a small fella. Didn't make it. That can't be him,' he said in disbelief.

The Boy in the Red Scrum Cap

'That's him, alright,' said the coach, laughing. 'He's a different beast now.'

'Certainly is,' said the scout, writing a few thoughts in his notebook. 'I think we'll need to have another look at him. A player like him is exactly who we need in the Leinster Academy.'

Chapter 8

Daydream Believer

When he wasn't playing rugby, Josh enjoyed spending time chilling at home with his family. He loved watching movies. *Star Wars* was his favourite. And he would often act out his favourite parts, running around the house pretending he was a Jedi Knight. He loved cowboy movies too.

But he could never sit still for long, and he'd soon be off again playing some other sport. He was a great cricket player too and spent many

Daydream Believer

summer evenings playing for the YMCA in Sandymount. He loved the sound of the bat on the ball and the long spells at the crease that tested your concentration. He was a talented bowler. He played a bit for the Leinster Schools team, along with George Dockrell, who would go on to play for Ireland. Perhaps Josh might have been good enough to play for Ireland too, if he had stuck at it. Or maybe his sister was simply better than him and he didn't want to admit it!

Golf was another sport that helped him switch off from rugby. He often headed for Wicklow Golf Club with his dad for a quick nine holes. He watched a lot of golf on TV, too. Ireland's Pádraig Harrington was one of the best players in the world when Josh was growing up. Josh tried to copy him on the golf course.

Josh was a bit of a daydreamer. And mostly his daydreams were about sport. When he was walking down to the shop to get some milk, he would pretend he was on a golf course, playing the winning shot at the Open.

Josh the Flyer

Josh van der Flier ... 150 yards from the green. He needs this to go in to win it ... Oh my goodness ... it's gone straight into the hole!

Or when he was tidying his bedroom, he dreamed of playing tennis at Wimbledon.

Van der Flier with a beautiful backhand ... Rafa Nadal has no response ... The young Irishman has shocked the world to win Wimbledon!

Even when he was on the way to training in the car, his mind was always wandering.

Josh van der Flier is straight through. He's heading for the try line to win the World Cup for Ireland ... Oh no! He's dropped the ball. The crowd are booing. How on earth did he do that?!

Sometimes his dreams were nightmares. But he liked that too. He thought a lot about how things might go on the rugby pitch. Good and bad. The important thing was how he reacted to disappointment. Even from an early age, he was already training his mind for success.

Daydream Believer

Sundays were a special day at home in the van der Flier household. The family would all gather and go to the local church in Wicklow. Then they would have a big meal together. Sometimes his grandparents would be there, or maybe a few cousins and friends. His family meant everything to him.

Josh loved reading children's stories from the bible when he was growing up and he said his prayers every night before he went to sleep. It always made him feel relaxed. He memorised many different verses from the bible.

One of his favourites read: 'Be strong and courageous. Do not be afraid; do not be discouraged, for the Lord your God will be with you wherever you go.'

Josh would repeat this in his head before he played a rugby match, or at other times when he was feeling sad or lonely. He believed his talent for rugby was a gift from God and it was up to him to work hard to make the most of it. He thanked God for all the good things in his

Josh the Flyer

life. But mostly he prayed for his rugby dreams to come true.

And it seemed God was listening.

One day that summer the postman popped a letter through the door. It was addressed to Josh. He never got post, so he was excited to open it. He slowly unfolded the paper. The page had a dark blue and bright yellow logo on the top corner. It was from Leinster Rugby. Josh's heart skipped a beat.

Dear Mr van der Flier, he read, as fast as he could, trying to get to the point. **We have great pleasure in inviting you to present for training with the Leinster Under-19 squad ...**

He didn't need to read any more details. He dropped the letter and screamed with joy.

'Yesssssss!' he shouted, pumping his fist into the air. He ran straight to tell his mam and dad.

This was it. The Leinster Academy. He was about to take his first steps as a professional rugby player.

Chapter 9

Leinster Life

Moving to the Leinster Academy was another big change in Josh's life. He had just finished his Leaving Cert and was about to start a degree in Sports Management at University College Dublin. But rugby was his focus now.

Josh moved into a house with other players his own age, who were also starting out at the Leinster Academy. They were Peter Dooley, Tom Daly and Adam Byrne. They were all so excited to begin their journey together. They were able to spend most of their time

Josh the Flyer

concentrating on rugby now and had three years in the Academy to make it into the Leinster senior team.

The boys had great fun together on and off the pitch. They learned how to cook and clean for themselves. They didn't have their parents around to look after them anymore. But Josh was used to that from boarding school. They were always slagging and joking with each other. Peter never moved off the couch. Tom took ages in the shower. Adam ate too loudly!

One of their favourite games was pitch and putt. Inside the house! They would set up a golf ball at the bottom of the stairs and try to chip it upstairs into the toilet bowl. It was so much fun. One day Josh missed the ball with a wild swing and took a lump out of the wall with the golf club. The lads all burst out laughing. No way would they have been allowed to do this if their mothers were around!

But the thing Josh loved most was how they all pushed each other to get better at rugby.

Leinster Life

They would chat about technique and tactics, make sure they ate the right food and not stay up too late. It was a great life.

Josh still felt he was one of the weaker players in the Academy. Although he had grown taller, this was another level again and he was still worried he wouldn't be strong enough to make the senior team. He even struggled to make the UCD team in the early days. He got nervous before games and couldn't play to his best. He decided to ask his coach Bobby Byrne for advice.

'I'm struggling a bit, Bobby,' said Josh, at a meeting in the coach's office.

'You're doing fine, Josh. Just stick with it,' said Bobby. He was delighted Josh had come to him. Sometimes young players hid their feelings and didn't talk to their coaches, family or friends about it. Josh had done the right thing by reaching out to his coach.

'It doesn't matter if you're not the strongest player on the pitch, Josh. You can always be smarter,' said Bobby. 'If you're smashing into

Josh the Flyer

a ruck with all your power, you still might not get the ball. But if you get there first, then you don't have to be strong. Do you see what I'm saying?'

It made sense to Josh. He just needed to relax and control his nerves. He was a fast, clever player. He just needed to play his own game and not worry so much.

'I think you might make a better 7 than an 8,' Bobby went on. 'You can play to your strengths. Take the pressure off ball carrying.'

Josh didn't have to think about it for long.

'Whatever you think is best, Bobby. I'd play anywhere to get in the team!' he said, laughing.

Josh had already moved from scrum-half to number 8. So switching to 7 was no big deal. He was willing to give it a go. Neither he nor Bobby knew at the time that this small positional switch would change the course of Josh's career.

'Thanks for the chat, Bobby,' said Josh, with a smile.

Leinster Life

'No worries,' replied Bobby. 'That's what I'm here for.'

Josh kept working away quietly. Learning all the time. Eventually he got his chance.

UCD were going well in the Bateman Cup competition. They beat Blackrock, Old Belvedere, Lansdowne, Old Wesley and Terenure College. Josh had forced his way into the team and was starting to make an impact. He was learning fast, playing against fully-grown men.

They played a tight semi-final against Galwegians in the west of Ireland. Josh's bright red scrum cap popped up all over the field. He was one of the standout players, as UCD held on for a 21–20 win. Unfortunately, they went on to lose the final to Cork Con. Josh was hugely disappointed. He had played well himself, but his team lost. He was making a habit of losing finals.

He thought his season was over and began thinking of a summer break. He was happy with the progress he had made on the rugby

Josh the Flyer

pitch. It was time now to concentrate on his studies for a few weeks and sit his exams. Or so he thought.

One morning, he was walking across the university campus when his phone rang. Josh didn't recognise the number.

'Josh, hi! It's Girvan Dempsey here,' said the voice on the phone.

Josh could barely speak. THE Girvan Dempsey. The legendary Leinster and Ireland full-back who was now working at the Academy.

'How's it going?' replied Josh, trying to play it cool.

'Listen, we're short a few bodies for training. Can you make it over?' said Girvan.

'Of course,' said Josh, delighted. 'I'll be there as soon as I can.'

Josh couldn't believe it. This was his chance. He was going to play with the big boys.

He decided to skip the lecture he was going to and head straight to training. But there was one problem. He had no boots!

Leinster Life

He quickly scampered around trying to find boots, asking everyone he knew. Eventually he was able to borrow a pair that fitted.

Phew!

He walked into the Leinster dressing room as quiet as a mouse, looking around at the players already there. Seán O'Brien, Jamie Heaslip, Shane Jennings. Some of his all-time heroes.

Josh got changed and headed out to the pitch, preparing for the biggest test of his life. A player came up to him to shake hands. Not just any player.

'Hi, I'm Brian!' he said.

It was Brian O'Driscoll. BOD. Ireland's greatest ever rugby player.

Years before, sitting on his dad's shoulders in the stands, Josh had watched Brian win a Triple Crown for Ireland. Now they were rubbing shoulders at training.

'I know who you are!' replied Josh. He felt a bit silly. Did he really belong here?

A few minutes into the training session, BOD popped a simple pass to Josh. But he dropped it.

Josh the Flyer

'Nooooo!' thought Josh to himself. 'What am I doing?'

'Come on, boys, focus!' shouted BOD.

Then it happened again. Another ball right into Josh's hands. Once more he fumbled it.

This was turning into a disaster! Josh felt himself going red. 'It's just nerves,' he reassured himself.

From then on, he did OK. Nothing spectacular. But he held his own.

'You did well today,' said Shane Jennings, as Josh walked off the pitch exhausted. 'Hopefully we'll see more of you.'

'Here's hoping!' said Josh.

It meant a lot to him to get praise from Jenno. He was a legendary Leinster number 7.

Josh had survived his first day training with the Leinster senior team. Now he wanted more. Luckily, the following year things got even better.

Chapter 10

Zebre

By the start of the next season, Josh was training every day with the senior team. He was improving every day and was starting to feel like he belonged. He was involved in Leinster's pre-season friendlies against Northampton and Ulster. Josh was really hoping this might be the year he would make his first appearance in the famous blue shirt. He wanted to catch the eye of Leinster's head coach, Matt O'Connor.

Josh the Flyer

One day after training, Matt pulled Josh aside.

'I hope it's not bad news,' thought Josh.

But he needn't have worried.

'You're starting at the weekend,' said Matt straight away. 'Don't get too excited. Just keep doing what you've been doing in training, and you'll do great. You deserve it.'

Josh felt a shiver go down his spine.

'Thanks, Coach!' said Josh with a smile. He played it cool. But he wanted to do a cartwheel in celebration right there. 'I won't let you down!'

Josh felt a warm feeling inside as he showered and changed. It was slowly starting to sink in. He was going to play for Leinster! For real.

The next match was against Italian side Zebre, away in the Stadio XXV Aprile in Parma, Italy. They were a young Leinster team, but they had plenty of experience too. Rob Kearney, Gordon D'Arcy and Ian Madigan were all starting for Leinster. Josh was number 7 and Jack Conan was number 8. Remember

Zebre

him? He was the giant forward for St Gerard's School, who had run riot against Josh's team Wesley back in their Junior Cup days. Josh had thought then that he never wanted to see Jack again. But now he was his teammate in the blue of Leinster. And he was extremely glad to be on the same side as him.

'We've come a long way from schools rugby to here,' said Jack.

'Yeah, for sure,' laughed Josh, as he tied up his famous red scrum cap. 'And we're just getting started.'

Before kick-off, Gordon D'Arcy had a word with Josh.

'Enjoy it! Take it all in. I've been here plenty of times, so I know how it feels. Just breathe and relax. You'll be fine!' he said calmly.

'Thanks, D'Arce,' said Josh. It meant a lot to get encouragement from one of the best players ever to play for Leinster and Ireland.

From the minute the first whistle blew, Josh knew he was in a fight. Zebre were a long way from being the best team in the league.

Josh the Flyer

But their forwards were faster and fitter than anyone Josh had come up against before. The whole game was moving at the speed of light. The pace and tempo were off the charts. Josh was trying to keep up. He finally got his hands on the ball and used his speed and strength to make a break.

The new kid in town, van der Flier, with a powerful surge. Leinster on the front foot!

The move broke down. But it helped Josh to settle.

It was lashing rain in Parma, making it a scrappy game. Nothing much happened until Zebre landed a penalty after 25 minutes, before Leinster's kicker Ian Madigan drew the sides level just before the break in a low-scoring match.

'Nice one, Mads!' shouted Josh, as the ball sailed over the bar.

Soon after the re-start, Leinster went in front. Mads was right at the heart of it again. He spotted a mismatch and glided past the defender, Bortolami. It was a race to the line now and Mads beat the cover to slide in.

A superb solo try from Ian Madigan!

'Yesssssss!' roared Josh.

It was a tight game, but Leinster had their noses in front. Then, 15 minutes from the end, scrum-half Luke McGrath slipped around the side of the Zebre defence unnoticed and touched down the try to seal the game.

McGrath! Where did he come from? That's the game for Leinster.

The final whistle blew. Josh raised his arms in the air. The Boys in Blue had won by 20 points to 3. It was a routine victory, Leinster's third of the season.

'Yes, Josh!' yelled Jamie Heaslip, walking off the pitch to put an arm around Josh. 'You never forget your first game. Excellent job!'

'Just glad to have survived,' said Josh, as he wiped mud from his face and took a deep breath. He was exhausted.

Ian Madigan grabbed all the headlines for his match-winning performance. But for Josh

Josh the Flyer

it was a moment to remember for the rest of his life. His first match for Leinster where he played a full 80 minutes. And a win too. Sometimes dreams do come true.

His dad made the trip to Italy to see Josh play. After all the years watching him in Wicklow, Dirk wasn't going to miss this one. He climbed over the barrier and jumped onto the pitch after the game to give Josh a big hug.

'That's my boy! Great game! I'm so proud of you,' he said.

'I've finally made it, Dad!' said Josh, with a tear in his eye.

He video-called home from the dressing room after the game. His mam, sisters and brother were all on the other end, waving and cheering at the screen. Josh smiled and laughed.

'Well done, Josh! Great game,' said his mam, blowing him a kiss.

Josh felt so proud. But he knew this was just a first step. Having done it once, he now wanted to do it all over again.

Chapter 11

Try Time!

Josh played six more games for Leinster in his first season. Things were going well and he seemed to be improving with every game he played. But the competition for places at Leinster was intense. Seán O'Brien, Jamie Heaslip, Rhys Ruddock, Jordi Murphy, Dominic Ryan, Jack Conan and Josh were all competing for just three spots on the team. It was a strange feeling for Josh. They were all friends and they helped each other every day to

Josh the Flyer

get better, all for the good of the team. But someone had to miss out on selection every week. It was tough. But that was the nature of professional sport.

The start of the new season opened a window of opportunity for Josh. Most of Leinster's stars were away playing for Ireland at the World Cup in England. So it was a chance for the younger players to shine. Leinster had a new head coach now. Matt O'Connor had left and had been replaced by Leo Cullen. Leo was a Leinster legend and he took a shine to Josh from the start. He offered him a senior contract. He was now a fully paid professional player on the Leinster team.

'Look, Josh, with all the other lads away at the World Cup, we're going to be relying on you a lot more this year,' said Leo, in a relaxed tone. 'I see how hard you work in training every day. It's time for you to kick on now. See how far you can go. Believe in yourself!'

Josh felt 10 feet tall. He had always admired Leo as a player and a coach. It meant the world to Josh that Leo was putting his trust in him. He wasn't going to let this chance pass.

Josh began the season in fine form, making the number 7 jersey his own. Leinster crushed Cardiff at home in the RDS arena in his first match. Josh played a fine game and his pal Jack Conan scored the all-important try.

Next up they destroyed the Dragons. They slipped up away to Scarlets, before beating Glasgow. Josh played every minute of every game and was starting to get plenty of attention. He was the talk of the Leinster fans.

'Van der Flier is one to watch!'

'He's playing out of his skin!'

'I never thought he would be that good!'

By now, Leinster's Ireland players had returned from the World Cup. So Josh had to settle for a place on the bench in the next game against Treviso. He was disappointed but understood he still had a long way to go to be the first name on the team sheet. At least he came on for the final 15 minutes, meaning he

Josh the Flyer

had now appeared in six games in a row. He was becoming a regular starter and now he was ready for the next step. The Champions Cup.

The Champions Cup was a huge part of Leinster's history. All the best teams from Ireland, England, Scotland, Wales, France and Italy took part. It was the one they all wanted to win and Leinster had a proud record. They had won it three times before, in 2009, 2011 and 2012. All while Josh was still in school. Now he was about to play his own part in the competition.

Leinster took a heavy beating against English team Wasps in their first match. Their next clash was against Bath in a must-win game. It was away from home in a famous stadium known as the Rec. It was a hostile place for opposing teams to play. An injury to Seán O'Brien opened up a place for Josh in the squad. He was starting on the bench. His first ever taste of Champions Cup rugby.

Johnny Sexton put Leinster on the scoreboard with an early penalty. But Bath hit

Try Time!

back. Their kicker George Forde landed two perfect shots to give his team a 6–3 lead at half-time.

But, midway through the second half, Leinster were in big trouble. Bath gave a huge shove in the scrum and Leinster's pack went backwards. The scrum collapsed and there were bodies everywhere. The referee raised his arm and blew his whistle.

A penalty try! Bath take the lead. And Leinster are looking at back-to-back defeats!

Leo looked at the bench.

'Right, Josh,' he said calmly. 'Get ready!'

Josh was coming on. He had 15 minutes to save Leinster. And he sprang right into action.

Leinster were rushing forward. Player after player smashing into contact. Suddenly, scrum-half Luke McGrath saw a chink of light. He picked up the ball quickly and fired a ferocious pass right to Josh. He was running at full speed right towards the line. But he still had work to do.

Josh the Flyer

McGrathhh ... Driven onto by van der Flierrrrr ... He's scored a try and Leinster have pulled it out of the bottom of the barrel!

Prop Jack McGrath and number 8 Jamie Heaslip were right beside Josh.

'Yeahhhhhhh!' screamed Heaslip as he thumped Josh on the back. But Josh kept his head down and ran straight back to the halfway line. It wasn't a time for celebration. This game was far from over.

Sure enough, there was more drama to come. The teams were level now into the dying seconds. But the referee signalled a penalty to Bath.

George Forde stepped up to take the last-minute kick to win the game.

He's done it. It's over. And Leinster's European dreams are over before they began!

Josh was crushed. 'Nooooooo!' he thought. It was happening again. Every time something went well for him, the team lost. What should

Try Time!

have been a day to remember had turned into a disaster. At least his first ever European try was something to take away from the day. But he would have preferred the team to win instead.

However, Josh's try-scoring performance against Bath had shown he could mix it with the best. There was no doubt now that he was an important player for Leinster. And he was back in the starting team for their next match against Ulster, where they bounced back with an 8–3 win. He started the next two Champions Cup matches against Toulon. But Leinster lost both, before a win over Munster at Christmas restored their confidence.

On a rainy night in Dublin, Josh scored his second try of the season against Connacht.

Leinster pounding the Connacht line … Going through the phases … And van der Flier dives over from close range!

Things weren't going great for Leinster. They were a long way short of where they wanted to be. But, personally, for Josh, things were going very well indeed.

Josh the Flyer

Everybody was sitting up and taking notice of the player in the red scrum cap. And it seemed only a matter of time before he would be called up for the Ireland squad.

Chapter 12

Ireland's Call

It was a cold January morning at Leinster's training ground when Josh got the call.

'Josh ... Joe Schmidt here.' The voice came through loud and clear.

Josh almost dropped the phone with shock. Joe Schmidt was the Ireland rugby team's head coach. It could only mean one thing.

'I'm going to name you in my Six Nations squad today. You've been a standout player for Leinster, and I think you're more than ready. Looking forward to seeing you.'

Josh the Flyer

Josh shook his head in disbelief. He was lost for words.

'Thanks, Joe,' was all he could manage to say.

Josh was quite emotional. Just two years before, he had thought he would never make it as a professional rugby player. Now he was going to play for Ireland in the Six Nations! Everything was happening so fast.

He immediately called his dad.

'Dad, I'm in the Ireland squad! I can't believe it!'

'Well done, Josh!' said his dad. 'I knew you could do it!'

'Will you tell everyone? Mam and all. Grandad?' said Josh quickly. He was so excited.

'Of course I will. Your grandad Johannes will be thrilled!' replied his dad.

'Yeah, he always told me to work hard and follow my dreams. That I'd get there in the end. I guess he was right!' said Josh with a smile.

'That's right, son. We're van der Fliers. That's what we do!' His dad laughed.

Ireland's Call

***

Josh was soon in the thick of the action. His first Ireland training session. He was filling in on the B team when he stepped into a ruck.

Smashhhhh!

'Owwwww!'

Josh was absolutely cleaned out by a huge hit. Like nothing he'd ever felt before.

Ireland's giant second row Paul O'Connell had hit him with a huge tackle. He was laughing. Josh didn't want him to know he was hurt.

'You'll have to try harder than that, Paulie!' he joked.

'That's the stuff,' said Paul O'Connell. The big Munster man was secretly impressed. 'This Josh lad is made of the right stuff,' he thought.

Things didn't go well for Ireland in their first two matches. They lost to France and Wales. So coach Joe Schmidt decided to make some changes for the next game against England. Josh got the nod to start at number 7. He

Josh the Flyer

was one of a few fresh players in the squad, including Stuart McCloskey and Ultan Dillane. That night, the players met for dinner.

'A song from the new boys!' shouted Johnny Sexton.

All the players cheered. Josh and the other new guys had no choice.

Josh stood up. He cleared his throat and sang his party piece: 'The Lion Sleeps Tonight'.

'In the jungle, the mighty jungle, the lion sleeps tonight ... Ooooooooo!'

The players laughed and whistled. It was great craic. Josh really felt part of the team.

Josh shared a room with Rob Kearney the night before his first game. He was a brilliant full-back who had played for Ireland many times. He told Josh to relax and enjoy the day, no matter what happened.

The match day came. Josh was nervous but excited. Games didn't come much bigger than this. Ireland v. England in the Six Nations. Twickenham Stadium in London. The home of English rugby. It was a baptism of fire.

Ireland's Call

Eighty thousand English fans were roaring before kick-off. Josh closed his eyes and said a quiet prayer. The biggest game of his life was about to begin.

It was a tight game, with neither side playing well. But then, at the start of the second half, Ireland took the lead. Scrum-half Conor Murray saw a gap and took his chance. He wriggled under the England defenders to touch the ball down over the line.

A tryyy for Ireland. Conor Murray!

'Yesss!' roared Josh.

'Long way to go yet!' replied Murray.

And he was right. Soon England were back in front. The flying winger Anthony Watson did the damage.

A looping pass for Watson... What a score!

Ireland worked hard to hold them out. Josh was tackling every white shirt he could see. But England quickly struck again on the other wing.

Mike Brown in acres of space. A knockout blow for Ireland!

Ireland needed a score. And fast.

Josh the Flyer

Ultan Dillane picked up the ball and drove through the England defence. Josh was on his shoulder and screamed for a pass. Dillane popped it to him, and Josh pumped his legs. But they were tackled close to the try line.

Minutes later, Josh got even closer. Ireland's forwards piled in near the English line with all their power. Josh picked up the ball and surged over the try line, touching down. His red scrum hat was all anyone could see as a mess of bodies lay on the ground.

Is it a try? Nobody can see if he touched it down!

Josh waited nervously as the video referee was called to decide. Had he scored a try in his first ever game for Ireland? He hoped he had.

No try!

The referee said he couldn't see Josh touching the ball down. He was devastated.

Ireland lost the game 21–10. Josh was so disappointed. No try and no win.

'Well played, Josh!' said Joe Schmidt, as he shook Josh's hand and walked off the pitch.

Ireland's Call

Josh saw his uncle and cousin in the stand as he left the field. He waved and smiled. Even though they'd lost, it was a day to remember. His first ever game for Ireland.

Josh kept his place in the team for Ireland's next match against Italy. It was at home in Lansdowne Road, where years before he had watched Ireland play while sitting on his dad's shoulders. Now he was out on the pitch, singing the national anthem. All his family and friends were in the crowd to watch. It was a special day. To make it even better, Ireland won 58–15. A huge win!

Josh had certainly made his mark. At the end of the season he was chosen as Ireland's Young Player of the Year. A huge honour. And, even better again, he was named in the Pro12 Dream Team. He had to pinch himself. Was this really happening?

The little scrum-half from Wicklow with the red scrum cap had made it to the very top of the game. And there was still much more to come.

Chapter 13

Soldier Field

Saturday, 5 November 2016, is a day that will live long in the history of Irish rugby. Ireland were playing New Zealand, the best team in the world, in an incredibly special test match in the famous Soldier Field stadium in Chicago in the USA. New Zealand were known as the All Blacks after the colour of their kit. Black jersey, black shorts, black socks.

In 111 years of trying, Ireland had never beaten them. They first played way back in

Soldier Field

1905 and in the 28 matches since, Ireland had never won.

Ireland travelled to Chicago in hope more than expectation. They had trained hard to prepare for the game. But New Zealand were much the better team. Nobody gave the men in green a chance.

Josh was picked for the squad and was named on the bench. Number 20. His Leinster teammate Jordi Murphy was starting at number 7. Josh was so excited. It was only his third ever cap for Ireland.

On the bus to the ground Josh was daydreaming as usual. He was hoping he would get a chance to come on and play a part against the All Blacks. He wanted to test himself against the best in the world. He looked out the window and couldn't believe the number of Irish fans outside the ground. The Irish squad were a long way from home in America, but still thousands of fans were there to cheer them on. It gave the whole team a huge boost.

Josh the Flyer

Inside the dressing room, coach Joe Schmidt handed out some last-minute instructions. He was from New Zealand himself. But you wouldn't know it. Today he was as Irish as anyone.

'It doesn't matter what anyone says before the game. It only matters what happens on the field,' he shouted, as he thumped his fist into his hand.

'Go toe-to-toe with them. Tackle everything in black. Smother them. Don't let them play!' he roared.

Josh was so pumped up, he wished he was starting. He had to keep his cool and wait for his chance.

The players could hear the crowd noise from inside the dressing room. They gathered in the tunnel, all very emotional. Just two weeks before the game, one of Ireland's best ever players, Anthony 'Axel' Foley, had died suddenly. It was a huge shock to everyone in Irish rugby. He was an enormous number 8 who was passionate about the game. He had

Soldier Field

played hundreds of times for Ireland and Munster and was a hero to so many. The Ireland team wanted to honour him in this special game.

The players gathered in a huddle.

'We all know what this game means,' said captain Rory Best. 'Give it your heart and soul. Don't take a backwards step,' he said firmly.

Munster lock Donnacha Ryan had tears in his eyes.

'I'll never be able to say how much Axel meant to me,' he said. 'He was a great man. So, let's do it for Anthony.'

The players made their way onto the pitch. There was a special feeling in the dressing room. To Josh, it felt like Ireland simply weren't going to lose today.

The noise in the stadium was deafening. It was a sea of green. Everywhere Josh looked he saw an Ireland flag, hat or scarf. He couldn't believe it.

They sang the national anthems. Then it was time for the Haka, a spiritual dance

Josh the Flyer

performed by the All Blacks before every game. It is one of the great sights in rugby. But not today. Ireland had their own tribute planned. The players in green lined up on the pitch in two circles. From the sky, it looked like a number 8, in memory of Anthony Foley. Josh believed Axel was looking down on them from heaven.

The stage was set for an epic contest. Now it was time to play.

Ireland were first to score. An early Johnny Sexton penalty settled the nerves. But it didn't last long. George Moala crossed for the opening try. New Zealand were in front.

Suddenly Ireland clicked into gear. A rolling maul thundered towards the All Blacks' try line. Jordi Murphy got his hands on the ball as the Ireland pack powered over.

It's hard to see the ball! But Ireland have scored! Jordi Murphy!

Everything was going perfectly for Ireland. It was a performance of accuracy, purpose and pace. Soon they scored again.

Soldier Field

Rob Kearney dancing a jig to the try line. He's stopped just short. C.J. Standerrrrr! What a try!

Josh watched on from the sideline. He couldn't believe his eyes. Ireland were thumping the All Blacks. He wished he was right in the thick of the action.

Suddenly Jordi Murphy turned his knee in a freak incident.

'Owwwwwww!'

Josh looked on in horror. But then he realised this meant he had to get ready. He was coming on.

He pulled up his socks and tied on his scrum cap. He didn't have a moment to think. It was his time to shine.

He immediately threw himself into tackles and ran like his life depended on it. He hit a ruck just inside the 22-metre line. The ball came free and, quick as a flash, scrum-half Conor Murray picked it up. There was a huge gap in the All Blacks' defence and he sailed right through.

Josh the Flyer

What a snipe from Conor Murray! He has the freedom of Chicago! This. Is. Un-be-lievable! Ireland lead by 17 points at half-time. Nobody saw that coming!

'Yes, Conor!' roared Josh, as Murray crossed the line. The crowd went wild. They were dancing and singing. The fans thought the game was already won. But Josh and his teammates knew better.

'It's only half-time, boys!' Joe Schmidt told them in the dressing room. 'They only need half a chance to get back in the game. Keep going!'

'Let's go, Josh!' shouted Jamie Heaslip, as he patted Josh on the back.

The second half was just as crazy. And soon Ireland were in dreamland.

Murray ... Works it away ... Sexton ... Zebo scores! Four tries for Ireland. Surely they'll win this game now!

But the All Blacks weren't giving up. The best teams in the world never do. They hadn't lost for the last 20 matches, so Josh knew they

Soldier Field

would throw everything at them now. He had to stand tall.

Sure enough, the black wave came. T.J. Perenara gave them hope with an easy try. Ireland were getting tired. Josh knew they had to hang on.

'Come on, boys!' he yelled.

But it was no good. The All Blacks came again. This time Ben Smith did the damage.

How did he get that away?! Ben Smith in the corner!

Then Scott Barrett came barrelling through Ireland's defence.

Ireland are on the ropes. They've blown a 22-point lead. The comeback is on!

Josh felt the game slipping away. The team had run themselves to a standstill. They had no more energy left. There was just five minutes to go.

'Dig in, boys!' screamed Jamie Heaslip.

Finally, Ireland got a chance of their own. They hadn't scored for most of the second half. It was now or never.

Josh the Flyer

Josh packed down for a scrum near the All Blacks' try line. He got down on his knees and prepared himself for a huge shove. He needed all his power and might to get Ireland over the line.

The ball popped out the back of the scrum and Heaslip picked it up.

'Go, Jamie!' roared Josh as his teammate broke away from the scrum. Heaslip thundered towards the try line and popped a perfect pass to the onrushing Robbie Henshaw.

Henshawww! Sees the line and goes for glory … He's over … It's a tryyyyyyy! Ireland have done it!

The players all piled in to celebrate. It was wild! The fans went crazy dancing and cheering.

Josh closed his eyes and took a deep breath. The referee blew the final whistle.

Rugby history … Ireland beat the All Blacks for the first time!

'Yesssss, Jamieeeee!' yelled Josh, as he collapsed into the arms of Jamie Heaslip.

Soldier Field

It was the hardest game of his life. But they had done it. Ireland had finally beaten the All Blacks.

During the celebrations, Joe Schmidt came over to Josh and shook his hand.

'You played a blinder, Josh,' he said with a smile.

'It's all just a blur!' said Josh in disbelief.

The players went on a lap of honour as the fans cheered them on. It was Josh's greatest moment on a rugby field. He would never forget the day Ireland beat the All Blacks and painted Chicago green.

Chapter 14

Work Hard and Dreams Come True

Josh was a regular starter for the Leinster team now. He played almost every game up until Christmas. He scored a try away to Glasgow, but Leinster lost. And he scored two tries in a man-of-the-match display against Ospreys. But, overall, it wasn't a great season for Leinster. Leo Cullen was still getting used to the job of head coach. They were trying to find the right mix of older, experienced players and young players like Josh.

Work Hard and Dreams Come True

Still, they made it to the knockout stages of the Champions Cup. Josh was on the bench for the semi-final against Wasps. He came on for the last 20 minutes in a 32–17 win. Jack Conan was among the try-scorers again, while Joey Carbery was man of the match.

Next up, they faced French giants Clermont in the semi-finals. Josh was disappointed to be left on the bench again. Dan Leavy was starting at number 7. He was a talented player and a good friend of Josh's. But Josh wished he had been picked instead of Dan. He found it hard to watch games from the sideline. He wanted to play.

It was a brilliant match. It was played in France and the Clermont fans always brought great noise and blue and yellow colours to games. Clermont were a formidable team and Leinster knew it would be a battle. They had lost to another French team, Toulon, two years before. Leinster always seemed to struggle against big strong French teams. And it was about to happen again.

Josh the Flyer

Leinster made a terrible start and Clermont took full advantage. They were 15–0 in front after just a few minutes. Josh was sitting beside his old Academy housemate Peter Dooley on the bench.

'We're in trouble here,' he said.

'Big time!' said Peter.

Johnny Sexton kicked four penalties in a row to give Leinster a chance, before a late try from another young Leinster star, Garry Ringrose. Josh played for the last 16 minutes. But Clermont held on for victory. It was a day to forget all round.

'Great try, Ringer!' said Josh to Garry Ringrose as they left the pitch.

'Too little, too late!' he replied.

'Yeah, these French teams are huge. It's hard to match their power. I don't know – will we ever beat them?' said Josh as he made his way to the dressing room. He was so disappointed.

A few weeks later Leinster played Scarlets in the semi-final of the Pro12. The game was

Work Hard and Dreams Come True

played in the RDS in Dublin, Leinster's home ground, where almost 16,000 fans cheered them on. Everybody expected Leinster to win. Nobody gave Scarlets a chance. This time Josh was in the starting team. But it didn't go to plan.

Leinster made a bad start once more and they never recovered. Ringrose and Conan scored tries for the Blues, but it was no good. They slumped to a 27–15 defeat. The Scarlets were into the final and Leinster were knocked out. It was one of their worst results ever. Josh and his teammates were disgusted. There was complete silence in the dressing room afterwards. Once again, Leinster finished the season empty-handed. All the effort was for nothing.

A few days after the game, Josh met up with his grandad Johannes in Wicklow. He was an old man now, past his ninetieth birthday, but still loved watching Josh play rugby. He cheered him on when he played for Wicklow as a boy, went to his school matches in Wesley

Josh the Flyer

and took immense pride when he played for Leinster and Ireland. He kept all the newspaper reports about Josh's matches. He cut them out and stuck them in a scrapbook. He was so proud of his grandson.

'I feel like I'm never going to win anything with Leinster,' said Josh glumly. 'Every time we get to a big game, it just feels like we're not good enough.'

'Oh, Josh!' said his grandad, putting his arm around his shoulder. 'There's only one thing you can do.'

'What's that?' asked Josh.

'Remember what I told you when you were a boy?' said his grandad with a smile. 'Keep working. If you don't get what you want, don't give up. Work harder and all your dreams will come true.'

'That's what van der Fliers do!' laughed Josh.

'Exactly,' replied his grandad.

Luckily for Josh he had a chance to finish a bad season on a high. Ireland were playing

Work Hard and Dreams Come True

a summer test match against Japan. Josh was picked for the team.

He had never been to Japan before. It was such an adventure. He loved experiencing the different sights, language and culture. It was different from anywhere he'd been before.

The game was played at the Ajinomoto Stadium in Tokyo. It was a warm and sticky day. Josh and his teammates lined up for the national anthems. There was a big crowd, and the noise was deafening. Josh had his arm around Garry Ringrose as they sang 'Ireland's Call'.

'I have a good feeling about today, Ringer!' said Josh as he tied up his boot laces.

'I hope you're right, Joshy,' said Garry, rubbing his hands together.

Ireland made the perfect start. Ringrose grabbed a wayward pass in midfield and raced away from 50 metres for the first try of the afternoon.

Ireland were too powerful for Japan. Soon Josh got in on the act.

Josh the Flyer

Quick hands from Devin Toner and Luke Marshall released Josh. He could see the try line but wasn't sure if he could make it. He thought of his grandad. 'Keep working and your dreams will come true.'

Josh van der Flier is powering towards the try line. He's pumping his legs. The Japanese defenders are trying to stop him. But he's too strong. He's over the line. It's a tryyyyy! Josh van der Flier has scored his first try for Ireland!

'Yesssssss, Joshy!' roared Garry Ringrose as he jumped on his back. 'You were right to have a good feeling about today!'

Josh was delighted. His first try for his country was a memorable moment.

Everything went well that day and Ireland won 35–13. They had a big celebration in Tokyo that night before travelling back to Ireland. Josh was delighted a bad season had ended well.

A few weeks later Josh got some sad news. His grandad Johannes had died. Josh went

Work Hard and Dreams Come True

home to Wicklow to be with his family. He was devastated.

After the funeral, Josh went up to his granny Joke and gave her a hug.

'I'm so sorry,' he said.

'Your grandad was so proud of you, Josh,' she said, giving him a kiss. 'And he died happy, knowing you had scored a try for Ireland.'

Josh smiled, even though he had tears in his eyes.

'He always told me if I worked hard my dreams would come true,' said Josh.

'That's right,' replied his granny. 'And now he's up in heaven looking down on you. And he'll help you every step of the way.'

Chapter 15

Knee Knock

Josh started the next season on a roll. He played five out of the first six games for Leinster in the new Pro14. He scored a try against Montpellier in the Champions Cup and they beat Glasgow and Exeter twice in a row. This was more like it for Leinster. Things were finally starting to click for Leo Cullen. They were back on form and Josh was one of their players of the season.

Their brilliant results continued over Christmas. Leinster beat old rivals Munster and

Knee Knock

Connacht. Then it was back to the Champions Cup where they beat Montpellier and Glasgow once more. The wins kept on coming and Josh was in the form of his life. Everything was going to plan as he joined up with Ireland for the Six Nations. He was certain to start now that he was playing so well. And Ireland had big hopes to win this year. They travelled to Paris for their first match against France.

They could hear the brass band playing from deep inside the stadium. Drums drumming, trumpets trumping and French fans singing along. Excitement was building in the Stade de France. It was a dark, wet winter's day in Paris. Just a few minutes to kick-off. To the start of the 2018 Six Nations. France v Ireland.

Josh looked around the dressing room. This place was as tough as it got in world rugby. Ireland never liked it. They had won just twice here in almost 40 years. Paris was a graveyard for Irish rugby dreams. But Josh felt this year would be different.

Josh the Flyer

Ireland were one of the best teams in the world now and they feared nobody. They had set their sights on winning the Grand Slam – the almost impossible task of beating England, Wales, Scotland and France in one season. In more than a hundred years they had only ever done it twice.

Josh nervously fiddled with his scrum cap, then looked up. His eyes settled on Rory Best, Ireland's inspirational captain and leader on the pitch, lacing up his boots. He looked across to Rob Kearney, one of the best full-backs to ever play for Ireland; to the Munster magician, Keith Earls, jogging on the spot. Then there was the new crop of young stars like himself, James Ryan and Jacob Stockdale, nervous but excited about what lay ahead. Coach Joe Schmidt was quietly dishing out some last-minute instructions. The tough teacher from New Zealand had transformed Irish rugby. Then came the referee's knock on the door. It was time. They all stopped and turned towards Johnny Sexton. Ireland's star out-half, the

Knee Knock

team's driving force and playmaker, the best number 10 in the world, with all the skills and a will to win.

'Let's go, boys!' he roared.

Josh felt a tingle run down his spine.

Fireworks crackled as they walked up the tunnel and out onto the pitch. The small pockets of Irish fans were making themselves heard, but they were mostly drowned out by the French. Almost 75,000 packed in for what was sure to be a classic. Little did they know they were about to see one of the greatest moments in the history of the game of rugby.

Josh stood still for the anthems. Then the referee blew his whistle and the game was on. It was fast and frantic. Josh threw himself into tackles.

It didn't take long before Ireland had a penalty. Johnny Sexton had the first shot on goal in the Six Nations.

A superb kick from Sexton. Ireland are in front!

'Well done, Johnny!' roared Josh.

Josh the Flyer

It was the perfect start. Johnny soon added another and Ireland were 6–0 up. Then France pulled back a penalty of their own. It was 6–3 heading towards half-time.

Ireland had possession and Josh called for the ball. He was clapping his hands and roaring at scrum-half Conor Murray.

'Yes, Conor!'

Josh started his run with a big French defender charging towards him. He went for a side-step, shifting his weight onto one leg and then back to the other. Suddenly, Josh's knee buckled under him.

'Owwwwwww!'

Josh collapsed with the pain. His teammates gathered around him as he lay on the ground with his head in his hands. The physio ran on.

'It's not good, Josh. You'll have to come off,' he said.

Josh was gutted. But all he could think about was the pain.

He spent the rest of the match on the sideline with an icepack on his knee. Ireland

Knee Knock

battled hard but with just minutes to go they were behind. It looked like they were going to lose. But then Johnny Sexton did something that nobody could believe. Josh could only watch and admire.

Three minutes and 42 seconds into overtime, Johnny looked up and gave Murray a flick of the eyebrows. That was all he needed. He scooped up the ball and fired a fizzing pass right into Johnny's hands. And then time slowed down.

Everybody could see what Johnny was going to do. The French players charged forward with their hands in the air to block the kick. The fans in the stadium couldn't believe their eyes. Surely he was too far out. Forty-two metres to be precise. It was one of the longest drop goals anyone had ever attempted. Everybody in Ireland watching on TV held their breath. Hearts stopped. It all happened in slow motion. Johnny had only half a second, maybe less. He released the ball and swung his boot with all the force he had.

Josh the Flyer

Sexton shows his guts and goes for glory!

Johnny gave the ball an almighty thump. The players froze. All they could do was watch. The egg-shaped ball flew high into the sky and started to spin ... once, twice, three times. It was on target alright. Johnny knew straight away. But did it have the distance?

Josh held his breath as the ball spun through the air. It was dropping, dropping, dropping.

Johnny's eyes bulged in disbelief. He was the first in the stadium to see.

It's going towards the posts ... It's gone towards the posts ... It's over! Ireland with the drop at goal. Le Drop! France have been destroyed with the final kick of the game. Ireland have snatched it!

Johnny stretched his arms out wide and pumped his fists in the air. He couldn't believe it. He'd done it. One of the greatest kicks of all time.

Knee Knock

Josh jumped up from the bench with excitement, before remembering his knee didn't work. His teammates went crazy, but Josh could only hobble towards the pitch. It was one of the greatest nights in Irish rugby. But it was a nightmare for Josh. He knew his knee injury was bad and that he would be out of action for some time.

The doctor confirmed Josh's worst fears. He had torn a ligament in his knee. He needed surgery and lots of recovery. He would be out of action for nine months. Josh knew he had a long road ahead.

He couldn't walk for the first few weeks after he came out of hospital. His leg was heavily bandaged and he had to put ice on it all the time. He spent his days playing PlayStation with the lads and a bit of Fortnite too. They had big tournaments of FIFA. Tom Daly was the best. Josh once had a losing streak of 21 games. He got a lot of slagging for that.

The doctor told him the most important thing was to stay positive. He told him to watch

Josh the Flyer

lots of funny movies and comedy shows and to only think good things. He had to imagine himself playing rugby again for Leinster and Ireland.

It was lonely at times. The other lads would head off to training but Josh was at home resting. He did a lot of daydreaming to pass the time. He often imagined he was a superhero, calling himself 'The Sidestepper.' He turned his cap backwards and made videos of himself singing his theme tune.

'Here comes the sidestepper!'

It was silly fun. But it helped him get through the tough times.

Soon he was back walking. Then cycling. Then slowly he was able to start jogging again. Every time he passed a new milestone, he would reward himself with a treat. Maybe a trip to the cinema. Or an ice cream! He worked hard with the physios and in the gym to build up his strength. He was able to work on his ball skills too. Even though he couldn't train properly he was still able to play with a ball.

Knee Knock

Throwing, catching, passing, even when he was just sitting on the couch.

Ireland went on to win the Six Nations that year. They beat Italy, Wales, Scotland and then England on St Patrick's Day to win the Grand Slam. History was made. But Josh played no further part.

To make it harder for Josh, Leinster continued their fine form without him, and finished the season by winning the Champions Cup. They beat French side Racing 92 by 15 points to 12 in a tense final played in the Spanish city of Bilbao. Josh cheered on his teammates from the stands and joined in the celebrations on the pitch.

'Well done, Leaves!' shouted Josh at Dan Leavy, who played a super game in the number 7 shirt in Josh's place.

'Well done, you!' replied Dan. 'You played a bigger part than me!'

'What do you mean?' asked Josh.

'Well, you played five games in the Champions Cup. And I only played three,' said

Josh the Flyer

Dan as he put his arm around Josh's shoulders. 'If we hadn't won all the matches you played, we never would have got to the final. So this medal is as much yours as mine!'

It was true. Josh had played a starring role in the group stages. And he now had a European Cup to his name. But it didn't feel the same. He didn't really feel part of it. Josh prayed that his knee would get better fast and that he would someday have another chance to play in a European final.

Chapter 16

A Famous Night in Dublin

Josh being Josh, he bounced back to action two months ahead of schedule. His knee was as good as new. Now he was itching to get back on the pitch for the start of the next season. His first match was against the Dragons at home at the RDS. Josh received a hero's welcome from the crowd. They were delighted to see him return. Soon he was on the score sheet.

Josh the Flyer

Leinster had a scrum five metres out from the Dragons' try line. They put on a huge shove and the ball came back to Jack Conan at the back of the scrum. He picked up the ball and charged to the line before popping a reverse pass right to Josh. He had the simplest run over the line.

It's a tryyyyy for Leinsterrrrr! Josh van der Flier on his return from injury!

'Joshyyyyy!' Robbie Henshaw slapped him on the back in congratulations.

'Good to have you back,' said Jack Conan, with a wink.

Leinster went on a winning streak. Josh played all the games as they beat Edinburgh, Connacht and Munster. He was rewarded for his fine form with a return to the Ireland squad for the November internationals. They were playing the All Blacks again, and this match would be in Dublin. Everyone was so excited. After the win in Chicago two years before, hopes were high that they could do it again. This time in front of their home fans for the first time ever.

A Famous Night in Dublin

It was a sparkling November night in Dublin. Cold and crisp. The atmosphere was building around town long before the kick-off. It was a huge game. The All Blacks, the World Champions, against Ireland, the Grand Slam Champions. It was a battle to become the number one team in the world. Josh felt sure it was going to be a magical night.

There was a fizz of electricity around the stadium as the teams walked out onto the pitch. Fireworks exploded as Josh and his teammates lined up along the red carpet, where they shook hands with the president. Then came the national anthems. Josh had been here before, many times. But this felt extra special. When he hurt his knee, he wondered if he would ever play rugby again. Now he was right back in the heart of the action. About to play the All Blacks in a game for the ages. He sang 'Ireland's Call' as loudly as he could. He could feel the pride surging through his veins.

And. Here. We. Go!

Josh the Flyer

The game was on. Josh jumped straight into action with thumping tackles, fine footwork and brilliant ball handling. He was a bundle of energy in an all-action display. The whole Ireland team was on song. But so too were the All Blacks. This was different from Chicago. It was a much tighter game. Both sides were fighting for every inch. Ireland were on top. But it was tight and tense. At half-time Ireland led 9–6 thanks to three penalties for Johnny Sexton. It was all to play for.

Then came the moment of the match. Ireland had a lineout near the halfway line. Josh stayed in the middle of the pitch. Ireland had a secret move, planned by coach Joe Schmidt. If it was going to work, it had to be inch perfect. Every player knew their job. Josh was to be a decoy. That meant he would pretend to run for the ball, but it would go somewhere else. The aim was to fool the All Blacks' defence.

The ball was thrown in. Peter O'Mahony rose highest to tap it down into the arms of

A Famous Night in Dublin

scrum-half Kieran Marmion. He whisked a quick pass to Sexton. Josh ran alongside Sexton as if he would get the next pass. But instead, Johnny flicked it back inside to Bundee Aki. He passed to Stockdale. The move was on ...

Ireland switch the point of the attack. Stockdale ... Chips it ... Will it work out? Will it work out?! The ball bounces ... Into the arms of Stockdale. He goes for the line. Stockdaaaaaaale!

The stadium exploded with noise. Cameras flashed and the players roared with delight.

'You pulled it off, Jaco!' shouted Josh to Jacob.

'I'll dream of that one for a long time,' said Jacob, laughing.

But the All Blacks never knew when they were beaten. They dragged the game back to 16–9 and pushed hard for more. They kept going into the dying moments, looking for a try to draw the match. Ireland were hanging on. Josh was thumping into every tackle.

The fans sang with all their might. 'Low lie ... the fields of Athenry!'

Josh the Flyer

Ireland's defence held strong. The All Blacks had nowhere to go. Eventually they dropped the ball. The game was over. Ireland had won.

A first ever win against the All Blacks on home soil. Everyone in the stadium would remember this night forever!

The Grand Slam heroes had done it again. Ireland had beaten the World Champions and were now, officially, the number one team in the world.

Josh looked to the skies. It had been a long road back from injury. But now it was all worthwhile. It was his best match in a green jersey so far. A special night in Dublin. A night he would never forget.

Chapter 17

Sophie

It was a memorable time for Josh off the field too. It was around this time that he first met Sophie, soon to become his girlfriend. He was on a night out with his Leinster teammates when he first spotted her. He thought she was beautiful. A while later they started chatting. They got on great, laughing and joking about all sorts of things. Later in the night she started to wonder if she recognised Josh.

'Do I know you from somewhere?' she asked Josh.

Josh the Flyer

'No, I'm just a student in UCD,' he told her, fibbing a little bit.

'But you're with all these huge guys. Are you part of a rugby team or something?' said Sophie, laughing.

Just then Bressie walked past. He was a famous musician in Ireland, who used to play rugby for Leinster.

'Hey, Josh!' he said.

Josh couldn't deny it anymore.

'I know him. That's Bressie!' said Sophie, smiling. 'You are a rugby player!'

There was no hiding now.

'I'm Josh,' he said, blushing.

'I'm Sophie! Nice to meet you!'

They got on really well together that night. And they soon began dating. The only problem was that Sophie was still studying and she was shortly heading off to Spain for a year.

'That's the end of that, then,' thought Josh to himself.

***

Sophie

Back on the rugby pitch, Josh continued his flying form with Leinster. They beat Bath twice, then Toulouse and Wasps in the Champions Cup. They were all set for another crack at the Six Nations. Ireland were hoping to follow up on last year's Grand Slam and the win over the All Blacks in Dublin. And what's more, the World Cup was coming up later in the year in Japan.

Josh had battled his way back into the team for the first match against England. But Ireland lost 20–32. Josh played his part as Ireland then beat Scotland and Italy. Next it was time to play France. A repeat of the match he hurt his knee in the year before. Unluckily for Josh, injury struck again. This time he tore his groin. He got lifted out of a ruck by one of the French players and fell to the ground with his legs out. The big French player fell on top of him and forced his legs into the splits position.

'Ouchhhhh!'

Josh was carried off early and missed another famous Ireland win. He was so upset. The doctor told him he needed surgery and

Josh the Flyer

would miss the rest of the season once more. But Josh had other ideas. He worked harder than ever and to everyone's surprise he made it back for the most important games at the end of the season.

Leinster were in the Pro14 semi-final against their old rivals Munster at the RDS. The fans couldn't believe it when they saw Josh's name on the team sheet.

'He's back!'

'I thought he was gone for the season. That's amazing!'

'How did he recover so quickly?'

It was all the talk in the stands before the game.

Leinster thumped Munster with a brilliant performance. Seán Cronin and James Lowe scored the tries, while Ross Byrne kicked four penalties and a conversion. But the best player on the pitch was Josh. It was a truly remarkable performance after such a long time out. He was presented with the Player of the Match award.

Sophie

'You're something else, Josh,' said Leinster's coach Leo Cullen afterwards.

'I suppose I'm lucky,' said Josh humbly.

'Luck has nothing to do with it,' replied Leo. 'It's your work ethic, Josh. You get what you deserve and you deserve all the credit today.'

Josh was thrilled. But there was one more big game left that season. The Grand Final against Glasgow. It was to be played at the 60,000-seater Celtic Park stadium, the home of Glasgow Celtic football team. It was a huge occasion.

Glasgow were a silky team with fast wingers and a dangerous full-back, Stuart Hogg. They flew into an early lead after just 13 minutes with a try from Matt Fagerson.

'Come on, boys! Keep the heads!' roared Josh to his teammates.

He had waited a long time to play in a final, so he certainly didn't want to lose it now.

Seconds later they were back in the match. Leinster charged down a Glasgow kick and Garry Ringrose was the quickest to react.

Josh the Flyer

The ball is bouncing. Ringrose! Leinster have scored a try. And it's a soft one!

Soon they were in again. This time Cian Healy did the honours.

Leinster were looking good. With just minutes to play they were in control, leading 18–10. But from nothing, Glasgow struck again.

Grant Stewart races away! And the final is still alive!

Josh was shocked. Was his final dream about to slip away?

'Keep going, lads!' he roared to his teammates.

It was nervous and tense. But eventually the final whistle blew. Leinster held on.

'Yes, Josh!' Johnny Sexton was first to congratulate Josh.

'Finally, I made it onto the pitch for a final,' said Josh, laughing.

This was one win that tasted sweeter than most. All his family had travelled over for the

Sophie

match. He hugged his mam and dad and then made his way to the stand to see someone incredibly special. Sophie. She had travelled from Spain specially to see the match. And Josh. They kissed and hugged and cheered Josh's success. He had been through two serious injuries but had bounced back. He had won silverware before, but this was the first time he was on the pitch for a final and got to join in the celebrations. Best of all he was falling in love with Sophie. He knew from that day on that she was the girl he wanted to marry.

Chapter 18

Rugby World Cup

The following autumn, Josh was off to Japan for the Rugby World Cup. He was thrilled to be travelling back to the place where he had scored his first try for his country. A lot had changed since then. He was an established player now and one of the first names on the team sheet for Ireland. They were considered the best team in the world and had huge hopes of winning the World Cup.

There was massive excitement in Tokyo when the airplane landed and the team arrived

Rugby World Cup

to pick up their luggage. Hundreds of Japanese school children waved Ireland flags and cheered for Josh and his teammates.

The players stayed in a city called Chiba, an hour away from Tokyo by train. There was a typhoon when they landed. A huge storm with high winds and lashing rain. Josh hoped it wasn't a bad sign for their World Cup hopes.

Their first match was against Scotland at the Yokohama International Stadium. It was full to the brim with thousands of noisy fans who had travelled all the way from Ireland and Scotland. The players were led onto the pitch by the sound of beating Japanese drums and then they sang their national anthems. Josh looked around and took a deep breath. This was it. The peak of any rugby player's career. What he had always dreamed of as a boy in Wicklow. Playing for Ireland at the World Cup.

Ireland made a perfect start. Their forwards were well on top. James Ryan soon smashed over the opening try.

Josh the Flyer

James Ryannnnn! Ireland are in front!

Next, captain Rory Best finished a powerful lineout maul to score again.

Ireland are in dreamland!

And it got even better. Scotland couldn't live with Ireland's power and soon Tadhg Furlong crashed through their defence. The same player who had smashed Josh playing for New Ross as a child was now his teammate at the World Cup.

It's totally one-sided! Ireland are too good!

Josh was so happy. He was about to win his first ever World Cup match.

Andrew Conway added another try for good luck in the second half.

Conway's dancing feet send him over in the corner!

Ireland wrapped up a 27–3 win. They were up and running.

'Great win, boys!' said coach Joe Schmidt in the dressing room afterwards. 'But don't get carried away. We're only getting started.'

Rugby World Cup

Ireland's next match was against the host nation Japan, in the Ecopa Stadium in Shizuoka. It was a huge occasion. Everybody in Japan was waiting for this match. They were considered outsiders for the tournament. But they had strong, fast players who could be extremely dangerous.

Josh felt a little nervous on the bus to the ground. The day was hot and sticky. He knew it would be hard for the Irish players to keep up with the Japanese.

There was a carnival atmosphere outside the stadium. The fans were laughing and joking together. The Japanese were in their red and white jerseys and the Irish were a sea of green. Young children were getting their faces painted. Green shamrocks for Ireland and pink cherry blossoms for Japan.

Ireland made another fast start. Jack Carty launched a high cross-field kick that fell into the arms of Garry Ringrose.

Brilliantly taken by Garry Ringrose!

'Yes, Ringer!' roared Josh. 'Great hands!'

Josh the Flyer

Japan hit back with a penalty. But Ireland came again. Carty launched another high ball and it fell back into the arms of Rob Kearney.

Kearney worms his way over the try line! He makes it by inches!

But that was as good as it got for Ireland. Japan kicked another two penalties to make it 12–9 at half-time. Soon things got unbelievably bad indeed.

Japan were attacking with purpose and pace. They were moving the ball from one side of the pitch to the other. Josh was struggling to get his breath. Japan were well on top and Ireland were in deep trouble. The home crowd were getting increasingly excited. Seconds later, Japan scored a try.

Japan have done it! Kenki Fukuoka has scored a try in the corner. Ireland are on the ropes. Are we about to see one of the biggest shocks in World Cup history?!

The crowd let out an ear-splitting roar. Josh rolled his eyes and put his hands on his hips. He didn't know what to do. They had

Rugby World Cup

just minutes to play to rescue their World Cup hopes. But everything was going wrong.

Ireland pushed hard for another try. But they had run out of gas. Josh had nothing left in his legs. Japan held out for a memorable 19–12 win.

In the land of the samurai ... Ireland have been put to the sword! Japan have caused a massive upset ... Nobody saw that coming ... Not even the Japanese!

Josh and his teammates didn't say a word. They were speechless. The dressing room was as quiet as a library. Their World Cup hopes were almost over before they had begun. It was Josh's worst day on a rugby pitch.

But there was little time for Josh to feel sorry for himself. Ireland had a quick turnaround before their next match against Russia. They won it 35–0. But even that didn't go to plan. It was another mediocre performance. Something just wasn't clicking.

Their last group game was against Samoa in Fukuoka. Ireland had a routine win by 47

Josh the Flyer

points to 5. They had restored a bit of pride and qualified for the quarter-finals. Now they would face the All Blacks once more. The team they had beaten in Chicago and Dublin.

Josh felt no fear. 'We've beaten them before, Ringer,' he said to Garry Ringrose in the team hotel. 'So we can do it again.'

The players were feeling the pressure. They had been together in camp for ages and they were a long way from home. They were starting to get a bit fed up of each other. Josh met up with Sophie and some of his family who had travelled over. He loved seeing Japanese culture. He visited historic sites like temples and gardens and tried the traditional Japanese raw fish called sushi. Back at the hotel, the players played table tennis and cards to take their mind off the big game.

Finally, the match day came. This was Ireland's last chance for glory. A knockout tie in Tokyo. All or nothing. Win or go home.

It turned out to be another day to forget. The All Blacks smashed Ireland from start to finish. Aaron Smith scored two early tries. Then came Beauden Barrett. By half-time Ireland were 22–0 down. There was no hope. Josh and his teammates had no answers.

It got even worse in the second half. New Zealand scored four more tries to romp to a 46–14 win.

The All Black machine is purring!

Ireland were simply blown away. Josh scratched his head and wondered where it had all gone wrong. Just a year before, Ireland had beaten the All Blacks to become the best team in the world. Now they were going home from the World Cup early. Josh was physically and emotionally drained. He just wanted to go home and take some time off. His World Cup dream had ended in bitter disappointment.

Chapter 19

Pandemic

Josh soon put his World Cup disappointment behind him. He bounced back in style for Leinster, starting every match as they went on a winning streak. He scored a try against Lyon in the Champions Cup and was in great shape heading into the start of another Six Nations.

First up was Scotland at home. It was Andy Farrell's debut game in charge as Ireland head coach. He had taken over from Joe Schmidt, who had finished up after the World Cup.

Pandemic

Josh knew Andy well. He had been Ireland's assistant coach before. Andy was building a new team, looking ahead to the next World Cup. So Josh was relieved to be picked to start the Scotland match. It meant he was part of Andy's plans.

Josh played well in a 19–12 win. Johnny Sexton scored a try and kicked all the points in a masterclass.

Next up was Wales at home. Ireland were full of confidence and started well. Two first-half tries gave them a 12–7 lead at half-time. Then they took charge of the game.

Hooker Rob Herring spun the ball into the lineout. It bounced back to Josh and Ireland set up a maul. The forwards piled around Josh, using all their power to push the Welsh pack away. Josh kept a firm grip on the ball.

'Yes, boys!' he screamed. 'Heave!'

They drove over the line and Josh touched the ball down. The referee couldn't see a thing. It was a mess of bodies. Irish players in green, Welsh players in red. Then Josh, in his red

Josh the Flyer

scrum cap, got trapped underneath. The video referee was called in.

'We can see clear grounding of the ball,' he announced.

'It's a try!' said the referee as he blew his whistle.

Josh pumped his fists and let out a roar. 'Yesssss!'

It was a huge score that helped Ireland win the game. It finished 24–14. Ireland now had two wins from two and were on course for a Triple Crown.

Their next match was against England at Twickenham. It was always a tough test but this one was tougher than most. It was a difficult day for Ireland from start to finish. They had no answer for England's power and strength. Josh came off after an hour. England were deserved winners on a score of 24–12, meaning Ireland's hopes of a Triple Crown were over.

Josh and his teammates sat silently in the dressing room afterwards. It was one of the heaviest beatings they had ever suffered.

Pandemic

Andy Farrell spoke to the players.

'Twickenham is a tough place to come,' he said with his loud, strong voice. 'But now you know what it takes. You must learn from your mistakes. If you learn and work hard to fix them, then we can all go places together. I believe in this team and what we can do.'

But just days later the world changed completely. Suddenly rugby was the last thing on Josh's mind.

The Covid-19 pandemic had started. It was a new virus that spread fast and made some people extremely sick. Everybody was scared and worried. People were told to stay at home. Everything closed. Shops, hairdressers, bars and restaurants. There was no school and many grown-ups had to work from home. It was a total lockdown. All sport was cancelled too. So, for Josh, that meant no matches and no training together with the team.

At first Josh didn't know what to do. He had just bought a new house and was living there with Peter, his old housemate from UCD,

Josh the Flyer

who was still his teammate. They had to train on their own at home, which meant they had to build their own gym. The garden was an overgrown mess, so Josh decided to tackle it by hand. He chopped down the trees with an axe and saw and dug the garden with a shovel. It was back-breaking work, but he had little else to do and it was great exercise!

Josh and Peter went running together to keep fit and sometimes saw some of their Leinster teammates out in the park too. But they weren't allowed to join in training together. Josh found it lonesome at times. He missed his family and he couldn't see Sophie.

The players joined video calls to keep up their spirits and have some craic with the lads. Leinster's coach Leo Cullen gave the players challenges too, to keep their minds active. They were given videos of other teams in action and asked how they would try to beat them. Josh loved trying to figure them out. Even though he couldn't train, he was still trying to improve himself as a player.

Pandemic

Josh and Peter played a lot of PlayStation and watched movies in the evenings. Anything to pass the time.

'Do you want some ice cream, Josh?' Peter asked him one evening.

'No, thanks!' said Josh. 'You know I don't eat rubbish.'

'Ah, go on! You're no craic,' laughed Peter. 'We don't have any matches. Who knows when we'll play again?'

But Josh refused to give in. He wanted to keep up his good habits of training hard, eating and sleeping well, no matter how much the world had changed.

After a couple of months, it was decided that professional sport could start again. Josh and his teammates were delighted. Matches were back. But things still weren't the same. There were lots of restrictions. The players could only mix with each other and nobody else. Strangest of all, there were no fans allowed to watch the games. Josh found it difficult to get used to and it started to affect

Josh the Flyer

his performance. He wasn't playing as well as before and he lost his starting place in the Leinster team.

A new young number 7, Will Connors, was starting to come through and he was playing well. It was a new challenge for Josh. He wondered if it was the end of the road.

But Josh knew what he had to do. The same thing he'd always done. Work harder. Get better.

He spoke to Leo and the other coaches. They told him to work on his tackling technique and how he entered the ruck. Ireland's coach Andy Farrell told him he had to be more selfish. He had to take responsibility for carrying the ball more himself. In the past, Josh had left that to the big guys. But now he realised he needed to do more.

He needed to be another option for his teammates when they were passing. He also learned to relax a little more. Before, he would always have his headphones on listening to music to get pumped up. But he decided to leave the headphones at home and chat to his

Pandemic

teammates instead. He found it much more relaxing.

The changes started to pay off. Josh found his form again. But Will responded too. They were both playing out of their skin. One week Will would play and get man of the match. The next week Josh would play and he would get man of the match.

'You're giving me a headache!' joked Leo Cullen to Josh and Will. 'If only I could pick the two of you!'

It was one of the things Josh loved most about playing for Leinster and Ireland. There was always someone waiting to take your place in the team. You could never let your standards slip. And that's what brings success.

With Will and Josh pushing each other to the limit, Leinster finished out the strange season in style. They beat Munster in the Pro14 semi-final. Will got man of the match. Josh was worried he wouldn't get back in the team.

But when the final came, Josh was picked to start, with Will on the bench. The game was

Josh the Flyer

played at an empty Aviva Stadium. Leinster won well by 27 points to 5. It was their third league title in a row. To make things better, Josh was named man of the match.

Josh and Will shared a hug on the pitch.

'Well played, Josh!' said Will, giving him a high five.

'We pushed each other all the way. That's what it's all about!' said Josh. The competition for their place had made both players better.

It was strange to celebrate in an empty stadium.

Peter came up to pat Josh on the back.

'It's weird having no fans here,' he said to Josh.

'Well, it's better than digging up trees and being stuck on the couch with you!' laughed Josh.

It had been a difficult year. But by the end of it, Josh was sure he had become a better player. Just how much better, he was about to find out.

Chapter 20

Triple Crown

The following year, crowds returned to stadiums and Josh was bang on form. In fact, he was better than ever. Ireland's first match of the season was against Japan in the Autumn Nations Cup. They smashed them by 60 points to 5 in a one-sided game and Josh was one of the best players on the pitch.

Ireland up and running ... A demolition of Japan!

Next up they faced the All Blacks once more. It was another classic match and Ireland powered to a 29–20 win. Josh tackled until he came to a standstill in one of the all-time great Irish performances.

It took Ireland 111 years to beat the All Blacks. Now they've done it three times in five years!

Then Argentina. Yet another day to remember for Josh.

Ireland were expected to win, but things weren't going so well after a nervy start. Josh helped steady the ship with a try from a rolling maul.

Here go Ireland with a big drive ... That's impressive from van der Flier!

And he did it again in the second half. This time Ireland were pushing forward in waves, smashing the Argentina line. Josh saw some space near the posts and screamed for the ball. Scrum-half Craig Casey threw a fast pass into Josh's hands and he powered it over from close range.

Van der Flier again ... He's been immense!

Triple Crown

Ireland won 53–7 to finish a perfect series. Josh had scored two tries.

'When I told you to be more selfish, I didn't mean to score all the tries!' joked Andy Farrell afterwards.

'Ha ha!' laughed Josh. 'I'm only getting started.'

***

Josh and his teammates loved playing for Andy and it was starting to show. The team was clicking into gear, and they were in decent shape heading to the Six Nations.

Ireland were up against Wales in the first match and they started with a bang.

Bundee Aki with a try after three minutes!

'What a start, Bundee!' yelled Josh.

Andrew Conway scored two tries and Garry Ringrose another, in a dominant 29–7 win. It was a super team performance.

They rolled on to Paris to face France in the next round. It was Josh's first match there since

Josh the Flyer

his bad knee injury and he was determined to do something special. It was a pulsating game. France scored in just the second minute. But Ireland soon struck back with a stunning try from Mack Hansen. He caught it right from the kick-off and ran through.

What a try from Mack Hansen!

Josh was first in to celebrate.

'How did you do that, Mack?' he asked in disbelief.

Before long though, Ireland were 22–7 down and looked to be in trouble. But Josh broke off the back of a trademark lineout maul and touched down for Ireland.

Clever play as ever from van der Flier. This Ireland team never know when they're beaten!

A try in Paris. Josh was thrilled. Three years earlier, his Grand Slam dreams had ended with an injury. Now he was back, better than ever.

In the end though, it wasn't Ireland's day. France were just too strong and squeezed out a 30–24 win.

Triple Crown

Josh and his teammates were disappointed. But Andy Farrell soon picked them up.

'I'm so proud of you, boys. That was a battling performance. There's still the Triple Crown to aim for. So, chin up!' he said, as he clapped his big hands together.

The games were coming thick and fast now. Ireland next welcomed Italy to Dublin. Josh was in the form of his life. He was everywhere in a 57–6 win and was named man of the match.

'Well deserved, Joshy!' said James Lowe afterwards.

'I don't know, Jamo,' replied Josh. 'You scored two tries!'

'Actually, yeah,' laughed James. 'That trophy should be mine!'

Things were getting serious now. Ireland were off to London next to play England at Twickenham. The last time Josh visited there with Ireland things had gone terribly wrong. But today was different. Ireland made another fast start. James Lowe had the first try.

Josh the Flyer

'You're on fire, Jamo!' shouted Josh, as they celebrated.

Hugo Keenan, Jack Conan and Finlay Bealham each added another try, as Ireland did a demolition job on England. The opposing team didn't even score a single try. The final score was 32–15. Now Ireland were all set for a Triple Crown decider against Scotland at home in Dublin.

***

On the day of the match, Josh was feeling calm but excited. He called his dad for a chat.

'Can you believe it, Dad?' said Josh. 'Ireland versus Scotland in a Triple Crown decider!'

'The exact same as the one I brought you to when you were a boy,' replied his dad. 'Do you remember it?'

'Of course I do,' said Josh. 'I remember every second of it. Gordon D'Arcy scored a try, and you lifted me onto your shoulders!'

'And now you'll be there on the pitch. Playing in the green jersey yourself,' said his dad proudly.

Triple Crown

'I have to pinch myself sometimes,' said Josh. 'All my dreams have come true!'

'Well, that's because you worked hard. You deserve all your success,' said his dad kindly. 'Now, go and win that Triple Crown!'

Lansdowne Road Stadium was packed, just as it had been 18 years earlier, when Josh had watched from the stand as a boy. Now he stood in the centre of the pitch before kick-off and said a quiet prayer. He felt everything was going to go right today. It was meant to be.

Ireland made a great start. Tries from Dan Sheehan and Cian Healy put them well ahead. But Scotland battled back. The crowd was nervy at half-time. Ireland were on top but couldn't get the score they needed.

They pushed even harder in the second half, pummelling the Scottish line. Josh covered every blade of grass on the pitch. Suddenly he found a bit of space.

Gibson-Park … Van der Flier … Josh van der Flier scores a try … Eventually the pressure tells!

Josh the Flyer

'Well done, Joshy!' shouted Jamison Gibson-Park.

'Some pass, Jemmy!' replied Josh.

Conor Murray added one more for luck in a thrilling finale. Ireland wrapped up the Triple Crown with a 26–5 win.

There were huge celebrations on the pitch afterwards. Andy Farrell gave Josh a strong hug. All the players were laughing and dancing. Josh waved at his family, friends and Sophie in the crowd.

When he was a boy sitting on his dad's shoulders, he'd watched and wondered what it would be like to win a Triple Crown in front of your home fans. He saw his heroes Ronan O'Gara, Brian O'Driscoll and Gordon D'Arcy celebrate that day. Now he had followed in their footsteps. It was beyond his wildest dreams.

The Triple Crown was Josh's greatest day in a green shirt so far. But he still felt he was only getting started.

Chapter 21

La Rochelle

Josh now had a taste for scoring tries and he wasn't about to stop. He took just seven minutes to score his, and Leinster's, first of the season against the Bulls at the Aviva Stadium in a stomping 31–3 win. And he kept it up all the way to the end of the season. He became a try-scoring machine.

Josh came alive in the Champions Cup.

He scored in the first match against Bath, helping Leinster to a healthy 45–20 win.

Josh the Flyer

Relentless Leinster ... Van der Flier crashes over!

Then he added two more tries at home to Montpellier in a whopping 89–7 win.

Van der Flier picks that one up. Van der Flier is clear again. And in he goooeeesss!

Conan ... Pops it up to van der Flier ... And that is out of the top drawer!

A few weeks later they sank Bath again in another one-sided game, this time away from home. Leinster were 64–7 winners and Josh was among the tries once more.

Henshaw ... van der Flier ... Runs a beautiful line ... And he's in!

Leinster saw off local rivals Connacht in the last 16 to set up a quarter-final against Leicester. And you've guessed it ... Josh scored again.

Larmour ... Quick hands to van der Flieeeeerrrrr!

He was in the zone. Leinster marched into the last-four with a 23–14 win.

La Rochelle

They came up against French giants Toulouse in the semi-final. It looked like a tough match on paper. But Leinster simply swatted them away. Josh played a starring role in a whopping 40–17 win.

Sexton ... One man to beat ... He's in ... He finds van der Flier ... It's a tryyyyy! There's just no stopping him!

It was a remarkable run. Six tries in seven games. Josh was one of the most talked about players in the game now. He had added try-scoring to his already impressive range of skills. He truly had become world class.

Now he wanted some silverware. He wanted a European Cup to add to his Triple Crown.

Standing in their way in the final was La Rochelle. The French side who had broken their hearts before, knocking Leinster out in the semi-final the previous year. They were a big, fit, feisty team and there was a real rivalry growing between them. They were coached by Ronan O'Gara, the legendary Munster and

Josh the Flyer

Ireland out-half, who would love nothing more than to beat Leinster in the final.

The game was played in Marseille in the south of France. Almost 60,000 fans were there, many of them travelling from Ireland to support Leinster. It was the most important game Josh had ever played for Leinster. He was out injured the last time Leinster won the European crown. He desperately wanted to make up for it.

It was a warm, sunny day and the noise was deafening as Josh pulled on his red scrum cap and tied it up.

'Let's go, boys!' he roared, just before kick-off.

Leinster made a solid start. Johnny Sexton kicked two early penalties to put them 6–0 ahead. But La Rochelle soon shot back with a try. It was a tight, tense game but Leinster kept plugging away. Josh did what he could to get on the ball and make something happen and he tackled his heart out, as always. Two more penalties before half-time saw them lead at the break, 12–7.

La Rochelle

'Don't let them bully you!' Leo Cullen told the players in the dressing room.

'Just keep going, boys, and we can win this!' said Josh, as the players huddled together.

Two more penalties from Johnny Sexton put them in control. It was 18–7 now, with 20 minutes to play.

'Yes, Johnny!' Josh pumped his fist as the ball sailed over. He was starting to dream of victory.

But unexpectedly, La Rochelle struck again. Their pack powered through Leinster's defence. Suddenly the gap was closing. Leinster were clinging on. Then the French side came again. Leinster were 21–17 ahead, with just minutes to play now. The worst lead in rugby. La Rochelle just needed a try to win it.

Leinster were trying to hold out for glory. They were hanging on. Josh was breathing heavily, sucking for air. The whole Leinster team were so tired they could hardly stand as La Rochelle powered forward repeatedly.

Josh the Flyer

'Come on, boys!' screamed Josh, trying to pump up his teammates for one final effort. But it was no good. Their defence crumbled.

Arthur Retière … It's a tryyyyy! Did he make it? By his fingernails … Against all odds, Ronan O'Gara's band of brothers have realised their European dream!

Josh slumped to the ground in disbelief. His European dream was over. Leinster had beaten everyone all season long. Josh had played the rugby of his life. But it had all come crashing down in the last minute of the last game. It was heart-breaking. Josh never wanted to see the black and yellow jerseys of La Rochelle again.

'Hard luck, Joshy.' His teammate Garry Ringrose patted him on the back.

'We'll get them next year!' said Josh, trying to keep his spirits up. But he wasn't so sure. He walked slowly down the tunnel and into the dressing room, where he sat with his head in his hands. Josh didn't want his epic season to finish on a low point like this.

La Rochelle

Luckily, he had one more chance to end on a high. Ireland were about to head Down Under to play a historic series against the All Blacks in New Zealand. Josh smelled another shot at success and soon he started plotting to pull off one of the trickiest tasks in world rugby.

Chapter 22

House of Pain

Josh was used to beating the All Blacks by now. He had played them five times with Ireland and won three. Few players could say that. But playing them on home soil was a different story. Ireland had never won a match in New Zealand before. In fact, only four teams in history had ever won a series in New Zealand. This was as tough as it got.

Josh was having the season of his life and the Ireland team was on the up. A series win in New Zealand would send a message to

House of Pain

everyone that Ireland were the best team in the world now. Josh couldn't wait. It was all he thought about on the long flight Down Under. He was ready to show the world just how good he had become.

The first test match took place in Eden Park in Auckland. It was a dark winter's night and the atmosphere in the stadium was electric. Josh took a deep breath and looked around.

'This is it, boys!' he called, clapping his hands.

The game was on and Ireland made a flying start.

Sexton to Ringrose ... Keith Earls ... Inside six minutes Ireland take the early lead!

But you can't keep the All Blacks down for long. Soon they were back in the match. And then they stretched their lead.

Sevu Reece ... They won't catch him. He can run through puddles without making a splash!

It was 28–5 at half-time. Not what Josh had planned at all. Ireland were giving New

Josh the Flyer

Zealand a tough game. But they couldn't match them on the scoreboard.

'Don't stand off them, boys! Get in their face!' Andy Farrell roared the instructions in the dressing room.

With his stern words ringing in their ears, Ireland hit back early in the second half.

Lowe ... To Ringrose ... Ireland have a lifeline!

Sadly, there was no epic comeback. Ireland gave it their all. It was a powerful performance, but the All Blacks kicked on and were soon out of sight. Ireland eventually lost 42–19. But the match was closer than the scoreboard suggested.

'Come on, boys!' said Andy Farrell, as the players gathered in a huddle. 'I'm proud of the fight you showed tonight. Yes, we lost. But I saw enough to show that we can do something special over the next two tests. We're still in this. Take the learnings and move on.'

Josh was disappointed with the defeat. But he felt the same. He knew Ireland weren't that

House of Pain

far away from the All Blacks. He knew they had a chance of making history and pulling off a famous win.

They had a week to prepare for the second test. Josh and his teammates watched videos of the first match to see where they had gone wrong. They listened to their coaches and trained hard all week. Before they knew it, game day had arrived. Josh couldn't wait to get out on the pitch.

The second test was played in Dunedin. The stadium was known as the 'House of Pain', where opposing teams came to get hurt. The All Blacks almost never lost there.

Just like the week before, Ireland made a fast start. With two and a half minutes on the clock, they scored the first try.

Sexton ... To Porter ... Charging to the line ... Oh yesss! It's game on!

Ireland went 10–0 up and were all over the All Blacks, dominating the game. Josh was having a huge influence, tackling everything in black. The only thing Ireland didn't do was

Josh the Flyer

add to the scoreboard. And soon they paid the price. Right before half-time, out of nowhere, the All Blacks struck back.

Beauden Barrett's got it ... Right on half-time! A sucker-punch for Ireland!

It was 10–7 at the break. Josh spoke in the dressing room.

'They had nothing the whole half. They got lucky. We have them on the run here!' he said.

'This is it, boys!' yelled Johnny Sexton, as they returned for the second half.

Soon they were back down near the New Zealand line, pushing for a try.

Porter stands over it. Had one already. Fancies another crack ...

Josh was standing right beside him.

'Go, Ports!' he roared.

Andrew Porter charged towards the line with Josh latching on to him, pushing with all the strength he had. He squeezed every last drop of energy out of his tired body to force Porter over the line.

House of Pain

He's done it! Ireland are on the edge of history!

'Yesssss!' screamed Josh. They had their noses in front now. They were nearly there.

Johnny Sexton added two more penalties for luck. Ireland had a 16-point lead now. Surely they wouldn't blow this one.

But the All Blacks didn't lie down. As ever, they kept going until the end. A late try set up a nervy finish.

Will Jordan pulls one back ... There's still time!

Josh looked at the clock. 'They can't score again,' he thought.

And he was right. Seconds later, the referee blew the final whistle. Ireland had done it. They won by 23 points to 12.

A famous Irish victory. Their first against the All Blacks in New Zealand. Their fourth overall!

Josh was too exhausted to celebrate. He put his arms around Tadhg Beirne. Andrew Porter joined in too.

Josh the Flyer

'Nice one, Ports!' said Josh, as he closed his eyes and sucked in some air. 'Two tries for a prop! Didn't see that coming!'

'Maybe I'll become a winger!' joked Andrew. 'We'll have some craic tonight!'

The players went crazy in the dressing room, dancing and singing. They had done something special that no Irish team had done before.

But they weren't finished yet.

Now that they had won a match, they wanted to take the series. It was one-all now. So it all came down to the third and final test in Wellington the following weekend.

Josh's mam and dad travelled over to New Zealand for the last match. It was a long way to go but they didn't want to miss it for the world. It's not every day your son gets a chance to make history.

Just minutes into the match they were extremely glad they had made the journey.

Ireland laid into New Zealand straight from the kick-off. They soon had an attacking lineout and Josh knew just what to do.

House of Pain

'You know the drill, boys!' said Josh, as the players gathered into a huddle.

They had practised the move many times before. Now it was time to pull it off. James Ryan rose highest in the lineout to catch the ball and pop it back to Josh. He set up a maul and Ireland were off, charging towards the All Black line.

This is a good heave. New Zealand are treading water. And Ireland are through again! Three Saturdays in a row. Three early tries. Josh van der Flier is the man who touches it down!

Josh's mam and dad jumped up and down and hugged each other in the stands. All the Irish fans went wild.

'Yes, Joshy!' roared James Ryan.

'I love it when a plan comes together!' laughed Josh.

Soon it got even better. Ireland scored again.

James Lowe ... Back into Hugo Keenannnnn! This third test is going very well for the tourists!

Then Johnny Sexton added a perfect penalty.

'Well done, Sexto!' shouted Josh.

Josh was having the game of his life. He was everywhere, pestering the New Zealand players every time they got the ball. It wasn't long before a third try came.

Sheehan ... Sexton ... Bundee Aki ... Over the line, Robbie Henshawwwwwww! Ireland are all over the All Blacks!

It was hard to believe. Ireland were 22–3 ahead at half-time. But they weren't getting carried away.

'We know how dangerous they are,' warned Andy Farrell at the break. 'Keep your heads. Keep going. We have them on the run,' he barked.

Just as everyone expected, the All Blacks hit back hard.

Ardie Savea touches down. It's game on again!

Then came another.

Rieko Ioane slips through the first tackle ... And the second ... Ioane pulls another one back!

Suddenly, the game was tied. Josh could feel another match slipping from his grasp. He ran faster, tackled harder and smashed into every ruck like his life depended on it. The whole Irish team played like never before. Finally, their reward came.

Good surge from Ireland ... Herring ... He stretches and he's got there! Can you believe it?!

Ireland were so close to victory now Josh could almost smell it. Then the referee finally blew the whistle. They had done it. History. An epic win.

Josh jumped for joy. The stadium erupted with noise. All the Irish players ran onto the pitch and danced in a group hug. Peter O'Mahony broke down in tears.

Look at what this means! So many talented teams have come here over the years. But none as special as this one!

Johnny Sexton was presented with the winning trophy and raised it high into the air. The players laughed, danced and sang on

Josh the Flyer

the pitch. Then Josh got an incredibly special award just for himself. He was announced as the player of the series. He couldn't believe it.

'Well deserved, Josh!' said Andy Farrell, as Josh walked up for the presentation.

Josh smiled from ear to ear. He picked out his mam and dad in the crowd and gave them a wave. They had tears in their eyes. So too did Josh. Ireland were back at the top of the rankings and Josh was on top of the world.

Chapter 23

Top of the World

Josh had won the Triple Crown with Ireland, become a try-scoring machine in Leinster's march to the Champions Cup final and played a starring role in Ireland's historic first test win in New Zealand. It was the stuff of dreams, and over the next few weeks the plaudits rolled in. He was named Leinster's player of the year, Ireland's player of the year and the European player of the year. He had scooped up all the awards going.

Josh the Flyer

There was only one way to top all that, he thought. He decided to ask Sophie to marry him. They had been together more than three years now. He loved her and knew he wanted to spend the rest of his life with her. So he finally worked up the courage to get down on one knee and pop the question.

'Will you marry me?' he asked her.

'Yes, of course!' answered Sophie with the biggest smile. The two of them cried tears of happiness and Josh placed a beautiful engagement ring on Sophie's finger. They were so happy.

Before the big day, Josh had a stag party with his teammates in Killarney in County Kerry. The home territory of Leinster's rivals Munster. They had lots to celebrate after a brilliant year. But, as ever, the lads had a few tricks up their sleeves. They made Josh wear a Munster jersey and a red scrum cap on the night out. Josh was so embarrassed he spent the whole evening hiding, hoping nobody would get a photo of him!

Top of the World

Soon it was time for his wedding day. The ceremony took place in the luxurious Luttrellstown Castle near Dublin. It was a beautiful sunny day and Josh and Sophie had all their family and friends there. Of all the wins for Ireland and Leinster, the tries scored and the celebrations, this was the happiest moment of Josh's life.

Afterwards, Josh and Sophie jetted off on a romantic honeymoon to Greece. It was the perfect way to relax.

He was having the time of his life. But there was still one more cherry on top to come.

At the end of the year, the World Rugby Awards took place in Monaco. Josh was invited to a lavish ceremony in the south of France. It was full of glitz and glamour. He wore a black-tie tuxedo and Sophie wore a beautiful dress. All the best players in the world were there. Josh had to pinch himself. He was sitting near All Black legends Dan Carter and Conrad Smith. South African star Bryan Habana was just a few rows away. They had been his

Josh the Flyer

heroes growing up. Now he was mixing with them.

He was enjoying the night, happy to be there, when he suddenly got the surprise of his life. It was time to give out the award for the best men's player in the world. The presenter stood on stage and opened the envelope.

And the winner is ... Josh van der Flier!

Josh almost collapsed with the shock.

'Is it me?' he asked Sophie in disbelief.

'Yes!' she said, with the biggest smile.

Josh slowly walked towards the stage to collect his prize. His mind was spinning. He thought back to his childhood, when he first picked up a rugby ball on the pitch in Wicklow. The games in the back garden with his dad and his brother. The advice from his grandfather to dream big, work hard and reach his potential. His school cup defeats at Wesley when he thought he would never grow big enough to make it as a rugby player. His early days at Leinster, his knee injury and his battles for a starting place in the team. Now, here he

Top of the World

was. The little boy in the red scrum cap, who everyone said was too small to make it, had become the best player in the world.

Chapter 24

Dublin Destiny

Josh didn't have too much time to enjoy the celebrations. The new season came around quickly, and Josh was raring to go. He was a marked man now as the freshly crowned world player of the year. Other teams would be making a special plan to stop him. But that didn't bother Josh. He just saw it as another challenge to overcome.

He continued his try-scoring form from the start of the season. Ireland backed up their

Dublin Destiny

win in New Zealand with home victories over South Africa and Australia. Josh was on the score sheet again. Now it was time for the Six Nations. Ireland were the number one team in the world. They had beaten New Zealand, Australia and South Africa, so they were setting their sights firmly on a Grand Slam. The almost impossible task of beating England, France, Wales, Scotland and Italy all in one season.

Ireland's first match was a tough test away to Wales. But they made short work of it. Just like against the All Blacks, a fast start did the damage. Two minutes in they put the first try on the board.

Sexton ... To Murray ... Sets Caelan Doris away and he goes crashing over ... What a start for Ireland!

Ireland's pack was far too powerful and soon James Ryan scored try number two.

Wales are shell-shocked!

Before halftime, Ireland were out of sight. James Lowe intercepted a loose pass and was on his way.

Josh the Flyer

Now we're going to find out how fast he is ... And the answer is fast enough ... Ireland are well on top!

Wales staged a revival in the second half and Ireland started to get a little nervy. But Josh popped up to settle things down with another trademark try.

Casey ... Pops it inside to Josh van der Flier who has all the space in Cardiff to touch down try number four. Ireland have won the game!

'Yes, Josh!' shouted Caelan Doris, as he tapped Josh on the head.

'We're up and running!' said Josh with a smile.

Next, Ireland faced France at home. The two favourites for the tournament clashing in Dublin. It was billed as a game for the ages and it didn't disappoint. From the first minute both sides went at it with fire and fury. It was a breathless game, one of the best anyone there had ever seen.

Ireland scored the first try.

Dublin Destiny

Beautiful ball ... Keenan ... Hugo Keenan is going to score for Ireland ... Oh my word!

But France fired back. It was end-to-end, tit-for-tat. Ireland edged ahead at half-time by 22 points to 16.

The second half was tight and tense. Ireland pushed hard but France gave them nothing. Josh was getting frustrated. The crowd were screaming Ireland on. Finally, Garry Ringrose found a way over the try line, and everyone could finally breathe.

Garry Ringrose ... He's in and over the line ... Finally, Ireland can celebrate. It's two wins from two. Is the Grand Slam on?!

'Well done, Ringer!' roared Josh, as he jumped on Garry's back. Josh knew this was their toughest game. But they still had to beat Italy, Scotland and England. There was a long way to go.

Ireland made no mistakes against Italy. They saw them off in Rome by a handy 34

Josh the Flyer

points to 20. They were building momentum now.

Next came a trip to Scotland. Always a tough task. Andy Farrell warned the Irish players to be wary before the match.

'These guys would love nothing more than to beat you today and end your Grand Slam hopes,' he said. 'Don't give them a sniff. I want you at it from the start!'

But that's not what happened. Instead, Scotland scored first. Ireland were getting worried. Mack Hansen steadied their nerves with a try before halftime. And in the second half James Lowe and Jack Conan added two more.

Conan over the line and Ireland can breathe a sigh of relief. They're just one win away from a Grand Slam!

'Great game, Jack!' said Josh afterwards. 'I thought we were in trouble there!'

'Never in doubt!' replied Jack Conan with a wink.

Now it all came down to the final match at home to England. A win there and Ireland

Dublin Destiny

would be the Grand Slam champions for just the fourth time ever.

Josh was busy in the run-up to the big game. It was the hottest event in town and everyone he knew was asking for tickets. But there was one person Josh wanted to be there more than most. His grandad George. He was old now and hadn't been to many of Josh's games in recent years. But this was a special occasion. It was not only a Grand Slam decider, but also Josh's fiftieth match for Ireland. So Josh and his family made every effort to get his grandad there.

Dublin was buzzing on the day of the match. It was the day after St Patrick's Day and everyone was talking about the game. The whole of Ireland had stopped to watch this match. It meant everything.

As the clock ticked down to kick-off, the dressing room was full of activity. Players tying up socks, taping their hands and icing their tired limbs. The sound of studs scraped the floor of the tunnel as the team made their way towards the pitch. They could hear a wave of

Josh the Flyer

noise from the stadium. Fifty thousand fans bursting with excitement.

Josh pulled on his famous red scrum cap and tied up the straps. The referee blew the whistle. The game was on!

Before long Ireland had a lineout in a dangerous place. Josh knew this was a huge chance. Hooker Dan Sheehan picked his spot and threw the ball in. A perfect spiral high into the sky, where the giant James Ryan leapt to catch it with both hands, quickly slipping it to Josh. It all happened in the blink of an eye and England didn't know what was happening.

Van der Flier ... Back inside ... Sheehan ... Gap opens ... Sheehaaaaaaannnnn!

Ireland have the opening try. And the place has gone wild!

'Yesssssss!' roared Josh. He was first in to celebrate. 'What a finish, Danno!'

'Wouldn't have happened without your perfect pass, Josh!'

It was a tough, tense match with neither side giving an inch. England were putting up a

Dublin Destiny

stubborn resistance and Ireland were getting worried. Josh was starting to wonder if his Grand Slam dreams were about to crumble.

Then, with 20 minutes to go, Ireland got their chance. Gibson-Park quickly fizzed a pass to the onrushing Bundee Aki. Bundee smashed into the English defenders and fell to the ground. Josh was first to the ball and forcefully shoved the English players out of the way. The ball came back again. This time Josh threw a dummy run that fooled England's defence. Bundee had the ball once more and popped it to Robbie Henshaw in space. The crowd roared in anticipation. Everyone watching at home held their breath.

'Go!' shouted Josh to Robbie. But he was already over the line. It all happened in a flash.

Can Ireland put the big man over? Yesssss! Robbie Henshaw! The power and precision of Ireland!

A superb try. But Josh and his teammates wanted more.

Josh the Flyer

Soon they were deep into England's half again.

Conan ... To Sheehan ... Ohhh, that is wonderful!! Try number two for Dan Sheehan!

Ireland were 15 points ahead now. But England still didn't give up. And they were soon back in the match. A rolling maul powered all the way over the try line. The men in white were right back in it.

'Nooooo!' thought Josh. 'It's too late to let this slip now!'

But there was one more twist in the story of this epic encounter. The men in green pushed their tired bodies into attack one last time. Josh, as ever, was right at the heart of it. Leading by example, showing his teammates the way to keep going. And eventually, England gave way.

Ireland are looking to put a cherry on top. Rob Herring! There it is ... The winning try!

It's a greenwash Grand Slam on St Patrick's weekend!

Dublin Destiny

Ireland are the Grand Slam champions!

The crowd erupted. Josh fell to his knees. He had done it. Ireland had done it. His finest moment on a rugby field.

The celebrations were wild. Fireworks crackled and music blared. The players danced and sang in a deafening din. Josh took a moment to break away from the party.

He made his way to the side of the pitch where his grandad George was waiting. He gave him a huge hug.

'I'm so proud of you,' said his grandad to Josh.

'Thanks for everything,' said Josh. 'You started it all. Rugby is in my blood and it's all thanks to you.'

Josh hugged his mam and dad. His sister and brother. His aunts and uncles were all there and Sophie joined in too. A Grand Slam win at home in Dublin was greater than anything he had achieved before.

Josh had gone from a schoolboy in Wicklow to a Grand Slam champion. The small scrum-

Josh the Flyer

half who almost didn't make it had become the best player in the world. The kid who ran around the house playing Cowboys and Indians had grown up to marry the woman of his dreams.

He was grateful for his family, who had given him the gift of sport and the work ethic to make the most of his talent. He wouldn't be here, he thought, without his close bond with his grandparents, who had given him the best start in life.

Josh looked out at the crowd, swaying and singing, all dressed in green. It was everything he had ever dreamed of. But he was hungry for more. The World Cup was just around the corner. He still wanted to finally beat La Rochelle and win a fifth European Star for Leinster. He had achieved so much but he still felt he had more to give.

Josh looked up to the sky and smiled to himself. He thought of his other grandad, Johannes, who had told him all his dreams would come true if he worked hard enough.

Dublin Destiny

Josh felt he was looking down on him from heaven with a smile.

'The best is yet to come,' thought Josh to himself. 'I just need to keep working hard ... After all, I'm a van der Flier. That's what we do.'

Also available

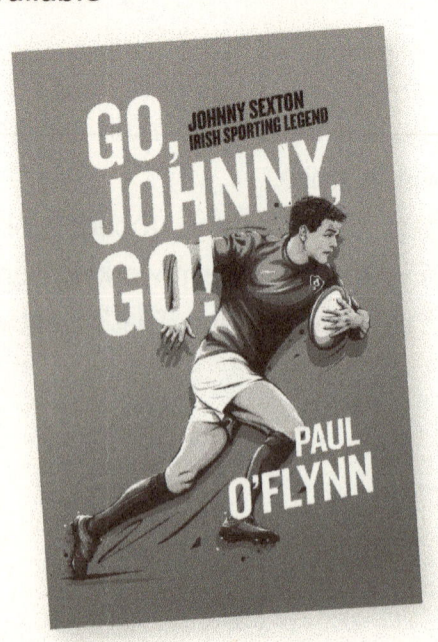

Johnny Sexton dreamed of becoming a rugby legend from the moment he was born. He enjoyed success from a young age, playing on school teams and donning the famous blue jersey of Leinster. There was one team he wanted to play for more than anything else: Ireland.

But someone was standing in his way. The Irish team already had a star fly half in Ronan O'Gara and he wasn't ready to give up his place. So began one of the great rivalries of Irish sport. Could Johnny go all the way to kick Ireland to grand slam glory?

Go, Johnny, Go is the incredible story of how Johnny Sexton became one of the greatest rugby players of all time.

Also available

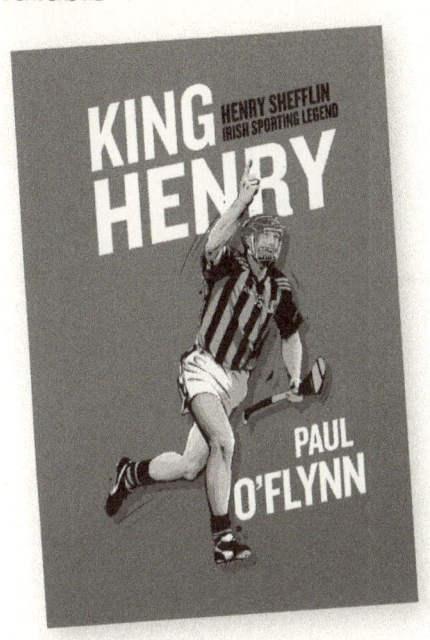

There are parts of Ireland where hurling is life. Luckily for young Henry Shefflin, his home village of Ballyhale in Co. Kilkenny is one such place. Henry is from a hurling stronghold where every thought is about the next point, the next goal, the next match. But there's only one match anyone talks about come September – the All-Ireland Final.

Can Henry be as good a hurler as his father and brothers? Can he train hard and overcome injuries and disappointments to one day play at Croke Park for his beloved county?

King Henry is the incredible story of how Henry Shefflin became the greatest hurling player of all time.